In Search of the Old Ones

In Search of the Old Ones

An Odyssey among Ancient Trees

Anthony D. Fredericks

Illustrations by Rebecca Noelle Purvis
and Phyllis Disher Fredericks

Smithsonian Books
Washington, DC

With love and respect for

my daughter, Rebecca, and son, Jonathan

Text © 2023 by Anthony D. Fredericks

Illustrations on pages 13, 46, 61, 72, 97, 109, 140, 163, 174, 187, and 198 © Phyllis Disher Fredericks

Illustrations on pages ii, 28–29, 32, 54, 64, 76–77, 80, 102, 124, 144, 164–165, 168, 180, and 194 © Rebecca Noelle Purvis

Published by Smithsonian Books
Director: Carolyn Gleason
Senior Editor: Jaime Schwender
Editor: Julie Huggins

Edited by Gregory McNamee
Designed by Gary Tooth

This book may be purchased for educational, business, or sales promotional use. For information, please write: Special Markets Department, Smithsonian Books, P.O. Box 37012, MRC 513, Washington, DC 20013

Library of Congress Cataloging-in-Publication Data

Names: Fredericks, Anthony D., author. | Purvis, Rebecca Noelle, illustrator. | Disher Fredericks, Phyllis, illustrator.
Title: In search of the old ones : an odyssey among ancient trees / Anthony D. Fredericks ; illustrations by Rebecca Noelle Purvis and Phyllis Disher Fredericks.
Description: Washington, DC : Smithsonian Books, [2023] | Includes bibliographical references and index.
Identifiers: LCCN 2023013351 | ISBN 9781588347473 (hardcover) | ISBN 9781588347480 (ebook)
Subjects: LCSH: Old growth forests—United States—Popular works. | Historic trees—United States—Popular works. | Conifers—United States—Popular works. | Trees—United States—Popular works.
Classification: LCC QH86 .F74 2023 | DDC 577.30973—dc23/eng/20230503
LC record available at https://lccn.loc.gov/2023013351

Printed in the United States of America on 30 percent post-consumer waste recycled paper

27 26 25 24 23   1 2 3 4 5

Contents

Preface

When an American reaches the age of one hundred, the president of the United States sends a birthday card. When a particularly long-lived person, such as France's 122-year-old Jeanne Calment, passes away, it makes international news. Even in cultures devoted to the young, we have long been fascinated with age and longevity. We tell stories of Ponce de León's quest for the mythical Fountain of Youth and of the biblical figure Methuselah, who supposedly lived to the ripe old age of 969. In fiction, we celebrate the mystical Shangri-La, a village where everyone lives well into their third century, and Brigadoon, where Scottish Highlanders hundreds of years old awaken once every century for a night of drinking and dancing.

That interest in age also extends to the protracted life spans of other species, both animals and plants. Those biological extremes often defy averages and open our eyes to some of the mysteries and little-known processes of nature. When we hear of a five-hundred-plus-year-old clam or an eighty-six-year-old elephant, we pay attention. As well we should, for organisms that live well past normal expectations are fitting sources of awe and wonder.

Ancient trees are a case in point.

There is no universally accepted definition of "ancient tree." The Woodland Trust (UK), for example, identifies ancient trees as those that "top the age charts at over 1,000 years." It has also posted three criteria for the "ancientness" of a given tree: it is in the third, or final, stage of its life; it is old relative to other trees of the same species; and it is interesting biologically, aesthetically, or culturally. The National Trust (UK), on the other hand, simply designates an ancient tree as "one which is remarkably old for its species."

We can define "ancient" as something belonging to the very distant past. But this begs the question: What exactly is the very distant past? How many years ago, what was the time frame, and what decades (or even centuries) were involved? Many of us took ancient history in high school or college, studying the rise of human civilizations over the last five thousand or so years. As you will discover in the first section of this book, trees inhabiting mountains in the American West, among other places, have lived for more than that span. I wonder, does that make them older than ancient history?

I think we can agree that there is a certain degree of ambiguity or confusion about the specifications that make a tree ancient. I suspect that much of the bewilderment about the term *ancient* is that the definition, quite often, varies depending upon the species of tree under consideration. For example, a silver birch, with an average life span of eighty to a hundred years, may be ancient at a century and a half. An English walnut, which can live for fifteen decades, would be ancient at two hundred years. A sequoia, with an average life span of two thousand years, would be ancient when it passes three thousand years. Although one thousand years is often the benchmark for "old" or "ancient" trees in general, the examples profiled in this book, such as the Bennett Juniper, all exceed that number and in several cases belong to whole species

considered ancient, such as Great Basin bristlecone pines
(*Pinus longaeva*).

The life span of trees depends on numerous factors, among
them climate, availability of soil nutrients, geographical location,
access to water, environmental challenges, fungal and insect
infections, forest fires, and human intervention. By those criteria,
we would expect an oak tree with easy and regular access to water
to live quite a bit longer than one suffering through a severe
drought over several decades. The bottom line, though, is really
genetics: each species of tree is "programmed" for a specific
lifetime—a life span ingrained in its genome and rooted in its
heritage. As much as we might want our favorite apple tree to live
for multiple decades by providing it with a constant infusion of
fertilizer, gallons of water, and lots of TLC, genetically speaking,
its life expectancy seldom exceeds thirty-five to forty-five years. Its
longevity is predetermined and preordained by its genetic makeup.

Let's take a closer look.

The more than five hundred varieties of evergreens, with
their characteristic year-round foliage and ability to tolerate
extremely cold conditions, evidence a wide range of life spans. For
example, ponderosa pines, common across the western United
States, may live to be five hundred years. On the other hand, the
eastern white pine lives no more than three hundred years, and
usually half that. For most of the common spruces, including the
Norway spruce and white spruce, the average life stretches from a
century and a half to two hundred years. Some blue spruces,
however, have been known to live for up to eight hundred years.
Coastal Douglas firs have famously long life spans, regularly living
for over five hundred years, with the oldest specimens exceeding
thirteen hundred years.

Fruit trees have similarly diverse life cycles. Peach trees
typically have a short life span of eight to fifteen years, although
some varieties, specifically dwarf peaches, can live for thirty to

forty years and still produce fruit. Plum trees will live on average for about twenty to thirty years, with some reaching an outside age of sixty years or more. Citrus trees have an average life span of about fifty years, with a few reaching the centenarian mark. Cherry trees will survive for an average of sixteen to twenty years. However, one species of black cherry can live for up to 250 years. In the wild, a pear tree has a life expectancy of about fifty years; Bradford pears, however, live for just fifteen to twenty years. One unique pear specimen—the Endicott Pear in Essex County, Massachusetts—was originally planted somewhere between 1628 and 1639. Having endured several hurricanes and an attack by vandals, it survives to this day.

Olive trees, cultivated since around 2500 BCE, will normally live for as much as five hundred years and still produce olives. Some olive trees can live for fifteen hundred years or more. The appendix describes two of these ancients; one of them, the Oliveira do Mouchão tree in Portugal, has lived for approximately 3,022–3,350 years.

Popular tree species, planted around homes and throughout neighborhoods, also demonstrate significant variations in life spans. These include American elms (average life span 150 years, maximum life span 300 years), eastern hemlocks (average life span 450 years, maximum life span 800 years), red maples (average life span 80–100 years, maximum life span 200 years), and white oaks (average life span 300 years, maximum life span 600 years).

In the course of my tree research, I also pondered the ultimate question about longevity: What is the oldest continuously living organism in the world? I eventually discovered, much to my astonishment, that scientists estimate a colony of *Actinomycetota*, a phylum of soil bacteria, recovered from Siberian permafrost to be between 400,000 and 600,000 years old. The miniscule organism is still releasing carbon dioxide gas as a byproduct of respiration, just as we do. Thus, this nearly half-million-year-old organism gives new meaning to the terms "long-lived" and "ancient."

In my pursuit of long-lived trees I generated another query: Where did trees come from? Or, more specifically, how did trees get started and how long have they been around? I began that quest in an arid dominion of northeastern Arizona.

I picked up the multicolored rock and held it gently in my hands. Slowly, I turned it over, entranced by the splashes of crimson, carmine, vermilion, amber, salmon, and peach deep within its interior. Its surface, reflecting the gleam of a summer sun, shone with intermittent splotches of lemon and scarlet. This singular stone was an artist's palette overflowing with pigments and light, a magnum opus conjuring the vibrancy of Monet, Van Gogh, or J. M. W. Turner.

This day, I was on an extended journey through the decorated canvas of the Petrified Forest. Here was a prehistoric environment, a rough and vibrant geography that extended far beyond the toothed edge of the horizon. Punctuating the terrain were multicolored aggregations of stone and rock, majestic and silent.

These are the remnants of prehistoric trees, *Araucarioxylon arizonicum*, stately conifers that dominated the Late Triassic (237–201.3 million years ago) landscape. They once lived when what we now know as the American Southwest lay somewhere in the middle of the Atlantic Ocean at the same latitude as present-day Panama. At that time, the continent of North America was separating from Africa and South America, a ponderous slip northwest toward its current position. The land was uncharacteristically tropical, a distinct climatic alteration from its present state.

An accident of nature preserved those ancient trees, a transformation into stone edifices sometimes rooted in the same positions they had occupied when alive. Most turned to stone through a process in which mineral matter, typically quartz, replaced much of their organic interiors. The trees kept their overall form, but the cellular structures were absent. These alterations took place over a long expanse of prehistoric time. What eventually resulted was a patina of geological colors across their faces and throughout their lengths. Here was an explosion of hues, blushes, and tints that tantalized the eyes with rich visions of another world.

This ancient forest is an impressive signature upon the surface of the Earth and an opportunity to discover something unknown and unexpected. Caressing a petrified titan poised over an ancient gully, capturing a multihued rock on my camera, or standing in wonderment before a pedestal log at Blue Mesa changed my perspective. I was reminded that trees are not just adornments of a landscape but also messengers of longevity and permanence. Even in death, they are memorials of arboreal significance.

The Petrified Forest is a monument to the lives and stories of ancient trees.

Let's shift backward to another time: the Devonian period, which began roughly 420 million years ago. Then, tempered ochers and muted crimsons washed the skies; blues were a rarity. Oxygen levels, a commandment for modern-day terrestrial and aquatic life, were depressed. Estimates of atmospheric CO_2 concentration during the Devonian was somewhere between 3,000 and 9,000 parts per million (ppm). Today, carbon dioxide concentration stands at approximately 420 ppm.

The Devonian was a time when a vast and turbulent sea bathed the planet and two trembling supercontinents, Gondwana and Euramerica, separated by the narrow Rheic Ocean, rumbled across from each other in the slow and patient waltz of tectonic plates. A massive subduction zone between the two geological beasts would eventually precipitate a major collision, joining the giants into a prodigious landmass famously known as Pangea. This was also a span of Earth's history when ascending sea levels created an abundance of warm shallow habitats. Sunlight, a necessity for the growth and proliferation of primordial marine life, penetrated idle waters dominated by jawless, armored fish, early sharks, and massive stromatolitic reefs veiled with cyanobacteria and red algae. Ammonoids, echinoderms, and trilobites also predominated as marine fauna diversified and migrated throughout this great uncharted ecosystem.

The land, however, was archaic and elemental. It was harsh and extremely poor in nutrients. Early terrestrial vegetation, initially spawned during the preceding Silurian period, existed primarily in wet environments, such as swamps. Spreading vegetatively, rather than by spores or seeds, these primitive organisms were short and scrawny. Unlike modern-day plants, they lacked roots; indeed, they had no mechanism to pull the surrounding waters into their systems. Predominate were the zosterophylls and trimerophytes, along with liverworts and mosses. Dense mats of *Cooksonia pertoni*, one of the oldest known vascular plants, crowded low-lying habitats with their slender leafless branches.

Then, about four hundred million years ago, many of these rudimentary plants developed a vascular tissue we now know as xylem (from the Greek word *xylon*, meaning "wood"). This tissue was revolutionary in that, for the first time, plants were able to move water from their base to their top. Over time, these new species developed a secondary layer of xylem, what we now know as wood. Although these plants were only about a half-foot in height, this early wood became a mechanism for the efficient transportation of water and for keeping an entire plant fully hydrated—a critical, though quite lethargic, transition in botanical evolution.

It would not be until the end of the Devonian, roughly 370 million years ago, that the first true trees would begin their ascent. These were progymnosperms, scientifically detailed as *Archaeopteris*, specimens that eventually rose to heights of ninety-eight feet (29.8 m) with trunk diameters in excess of three feet (0.9 m). Spread across their elementary "branches" were fernlike structures that, although lacking the stems of true leaves, gave these stalwarts a decided treelike feature: they were deciduous.

The woody roots of *Archaeopteris* helped these plants anchor themselves in the earth and to stay hydrated. That constant hydration allowed these trees to migrate away from swampy landscapes and, in turn, develop new ways of reproduction. Since they no longer needed ideal environmental conditions for reproduction, they were able to spread into new territories and ecosystems. Thus fossils of *Archaeopteris* have been found on every continent, including Antarctica.

In February 2020, eleven scientists from the United States and England reported the discovery of, arguably, the world's oldest forest, a congregation of *Archaeopteris* trees in an abandoned quarry outside Cairo, New York. Scientifically dated at 385 million years old, the fossilized roots of dozens of these ancient trees highlight a critical, though lengthy, juncture in the biological history of the Earth: the capture of CO_2, carbon dioxide, and the production of O_2, oxygen. The patient evolution of *Archaeopteris* meant that carbon dioxide was ever so slowly captured and locked away. In turn, the Earth's atmosphere began a historic and altering shift, allowing for a concomitant rise in oxygen levels and an atmosphere conducive to the expansion of multiple forms of life. *Archaeopteris*, along with its evolutionary relatives, helped create an environment that eventually allowed higher forms of life, such as early hominins (2.8 million years ago), to exist and

evolve. In short, we were, and we continue to be, dependent
on trees.

Just as I experienced the fossilized fragments of *Araucarioxylon
arizonicum* extant when the age of dinosaurs was just beginning,
so too did I discover other sites that have revealed significant
elements of arboreal history. Discoveries within those sites have
expanded our appreciation of trees as commanding elements of
the natural world. Experiencing their existence is quite often a
voyage into the processes of time.

In the coal fields of Kentucky lie fossilized tree stumps
entombed in Pennsylvanian rocks (299 to 323 million years ago).
Among them are lycopods, the most common fossil tree stumps
preserved in the Bluegrass State. What makes these trees particularly distinctive is that they did not have woody tissues; instead,
more than three-quarters of the trunk was composed of bark.
Calamites, reedlike plants, are also a common fossil tree preserved
throughout these enormous coal fields. Although some grew to the
heights of small trees, most rose to heights of only roughly three
to five feet (0.9–1.5 m). They tended to occupy riparian habitats
(e.g. river and lake margins, wetlands, floodplains). Cordaite trees,
a type of gymnosperm, were also prevalent during the Pennsylvanian period. Although no known Cordaites stumps have been
documented in Kentucky, their leaves have been found in some
shales and coaly strata throughout the state.

A discovery in the Mancos Shale Formation of central Utah
in 2014 confirms the existence of towering angiosperms throughout North America some ninety-two million years ago, fifteen
million years before the next oldest North American fossils of large
flowering trees. There, scientists discovered mineralized remains
of a log measuring about six feet (1.8 m) wide and thirty-six feet

(11 m) long. Site calculations indicate that the original tree stood about 170 feet (51.8 m) tall, more than twice as high as the tallest living tree in Utah today, an eighty-three-foot (25.4 m)-tall cottonwood tree in Zion National Park. According to the researchers, this fossil tree trunk, most likely a member of *Paraphyllanthoxylon*, an extinct genus, is one of the earliest documented occurrences of an angiosperm tree. We know that flowering plants arose approximately 135 million years ago. This fossil is clear evidence that those early North American angiosperms eventually evolved into ascending trees about forty-five million years later.

The Florissant Fossil Beds National Monument near Florissant, Colorado, preserves terrestrial biota that lived thirty-four million years ago. Within the monument are the petrified remains of massive redwood trees that once dominated the Eocene-Oligocene landscape. One of the most notable is the "Redwood trio," the only known fossil occurrence of a redwood "family circle." It and the other redwood fossils in the Monument are confirmation that these trees have a long and protracted history. Today's redwood species—coast redwoods, giant sequoias, and China's dawn redwoods—are descendants of a group of conifers, according to the Save the Redwoods League, that once flourished more than 144 million years ago during the Cretaceous period. At that time, the Earth's climate was warmer and more humid than it is today, so redwood species grew across multiple continents. Over time, and in response to ever-changing environmental conditions, they retreated from most of their former range. As a result, many once-abundant redwood species became extinct. Successive ice ages, including the most recent one ending about 11,700 years ago, eventually restricted the remaining redwood species to three small, distinct regions primarily in California and Sichuan Province in China. Their memories, however, are well preserved.

Arguably one of the most significant of ancient trees, one still living today, is *Ginkgo biloba*. A member of the order

Ginkgoales, ginkgos first appeared more than 290 million years ago during the Permian period (298.9–251.9 Mya). Fossilized remains of this tree have been traced to the Middle Jurassic period, approximately 170 million years ago. In short, ginkgos were extant long before the age of dinosaurs, through multiple mass extinctions, and across several ice ages. Thus, its botanical nickname: "living fossil."

Over the years, reports in numerous periodicals have posited that ginkgos may be almost immortal. Published reports suggest that individual trees can live to upward of a thousand years, along with unconfirmed accounts of two-thousand- and three-thousand-year-old trees. A study conducted by a team of sixteen Chinese scientists and published in *Proceedings of the National Academy of Sciences* gives scientific substance to the notion that this species may well be the grand champion of old trees. During their research, the scientists focused on the tree's vascular cambium, a thin layer of tissue that produces new bark and wood. In turn, they examined the cambium activity, hormone levels, resistance-associated genes, and factors connected to cell death. As they reported in their study, transcriptomic analysis (biological investigation of cell cultures with regard to growth rates and productivity) indicated that the vascular cambium of the oldest trees exhibited no evidence of senescence, the gradual deterioration of functional characteristics in living organisms, also known as biological aging. In addition, they concluded that the vascular cambium in *Ginkgo biloba* can retain the capacity for continuous growth for hundreds of years or even millennia.

This is not to say that these trees are eternally immortal, just that they typically do not succumb to old age. Their demise is often the result of external factors such as fire, disease, lightning, harsh winds, or even, excessive logging. As the scientists report, "extensive expression of genes associated with preformed and inducible defenses likely contributes to the remarkable longevity of this species." In short, this tree has survived the ages with extraordinary vigor and endurance. Its currency is well rooted in ancient times.

Determining the age of trees, particularly old trees, is often a multifaceted process. Dendrochronologists, scientists who work to date trees and, often, human artifacts and buildings found in association with those trees, frequently rely on two primary methods. The best known is to count tree rings (also known as growth rings) via increment boring to determine the exact year a tree was formed. The boring process removes a pencil-like core from the exterior to interior of a tree—a core that reveals the tree's rings. Each ring in the trunk of a tree marks a complete cycle of seasons, or one year, in the tree's life. And so, counting backward from the outer bark to the heartwood, those scientists can be quite specific (assuming, of course, that they know what year the tree was cut down). As well as determining the overall age of a tree, this method provides scientific data for dendroclimatology, the study of climate and atmospheric conditions during different periods in the tree's history.

Not surprisingly, old trees sometimes harbor rotted wood or vanished centers. This may be the result of fungal attacks, very wet conditions over long periods of time, severe climatological variations, insect infestation, or disease. As a result, dendrochronologists may have to estimate a delicate tree's age by taking a core and extrapolating past the recorded rings. In times past, these cores were so large and invasive that the tree being censused all too often died despite scientists' efforts to cause it no harm. Now dendrochronologists liken coring to our getting a flu shot, with a thin but long drill bit inserted into the tree to obtain a complete ring sequence.

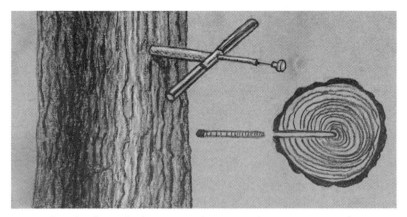

Dendrochronologists use an increment borer to accurately
determine the age of a tree.

Radiocarbon dating is an alternate method for determining
the age of a deceased organism such as a tree. That process
measures the half-life of carbon-14 (C-14), a radioactive isotope of
carbon present in all living organisms. (Half-life refers to the time
it takes for half of a given element to decay.) Typically, half of C-14
decays every $5,730 \pm 40$ years. Thus, scientists can measure the
amount of C-14 left in a dead organism, the result of which will
indicate how long ago it stopped exchanging carbon with
the atmosphere.

Radiocarbon dating is particularly useful for deceased
specimens whose ages may go back several thousands of years. For
example, the radiocarbon dating of dead samples of Great Basin
bristlecone pines (in concert with the dating of live trees) in the
White Mountains of California made possible a long, unbroken
tree ring sequence dating back about eleven thousand years (which
we denote numerically as ~11,000).

Several years ago, while pursuing research for *The Secret Life
of Clams*, I discovered that counting rings is not the exclusive
province of dendrochronologists. Annual growth rings are used by

some scientists (in this case, sclerochronologists) to determine ancient climates as well as the age of select marine organisms.

In 2006, scientists from Bangor University in England were conducting undersea research near Iceland as part of a long-term climatological project. In the process of retrieving deep water clams, they pulled up an undistinguished *Arctica islandica*. After it arrived at the laboratory, its growth rings (on the inside of the shell) were methodically counted. This was done because the rings there are better protected and thus less subject to the wear and tear that might occur on the outside of the shell. The scientists came up with an initial figure of 405 years.

The specimen was tagged with the designation "Tree of the Sea" in homage to the growth increment series measured from its shells that was used retrospectively to reconstruct marine environmental change. Chris Richardson, from the University's School of Ocean Sciences, told the BBC, "The growth-increments themselves provide a record of how the animal has varied in its growth-rate from year to year, and that varies according to climate, sea-water temperature, and food supply."

In 2013, the scientists decided to do a recount, carefully calculating the number of rings on the outside of the shell. The results indicated that the clam was actually 507 years old, not 405 years old as originally thought. "We got it wrong the first time and maybe we were a bit [hasty] publishing our findings back then. But we are absolutely certain that we've got the right age now," said scientist Paul Butler.

Consider this: at 507 years old, this oldster, nicknamed "Ming," lived from the year 1499 until the day sclerochronologists opened its shells in 2006 to count its rings. It "settled," was born, in the same year that Switzerland became an independent state (September 22, 1499), just before Pedro Álvares Cabral officially discovered Brazil and claim the land for Portugal (April 22, 1500), and just after Columbus's third voyage to the New World (May–August 1498).

Microns of calcite and aragonite had been laid down in concentric arcs across the shell of this deep-water denizen, each a measure of temperature, salinity, volcanic disturbances, nutritional availability, climatic alterations, currents, and, of course, an extended life. Like tree rings, these were markers of time and existence; measurements of ecology quite often beyond human perception. In short, rings of life. Although a "mere" clam, it lays claim as the longest-lived animal in the world.

Dendrochronologists and sclerochronologists are not the only scientists who determine an organism's age via growth rings. Ichthyologists can determine the age of a fish by counting growth rings on its scales or on its otoliths (ear bones). The rings represent seasonal changes in the growth of a fish.

Measuring growth rings is critical in understanding the lives of both plants and animals. Dendrochronology provides important data in any discussion of ancient trees. Thus, the two primary methodologies (increment boring and radiocarbon dating) for dating trees figure throughout the book. They will help us to get a sense of the "ancientness" of a forest or an individual tree by way of scientifically accepted protocols instead of guesswork. In the future, specific ages of those trees may change as we develop new methods of measurement, improved instruments, and the like, all of which help us inch a little closer to the truth—which is the very nature of scientific research.

Introduction

Resolute sentinels of time, trees consistently engender admiration
and affection. There are something like three trillion of them (or
approximately 422 trees for every person on Earth), and more
than sixty thousand species. Generations of botanists both
amateur and professional have celebrated trees as sources of
wisdom, sacred beings, and metaphors for youth and old age, as
well as for their solidity and sagacity, their ancestral roots and
evolutionary resilience. Saints, emperors, and despots have
consulted trees, seeking their guidance. Commoners and poets
have praised them, and people in every precinct, county, province, and political jurisdiction across the globe rightly admire
trees. Pantheons around the world have included tree spirits,
druids, and forest gods among their sacred beings.

Trees are graceful, muscular, and quite often just plain
magnificent. We have built our shelters in them, with them, and
among them. In Africa, baobab trees have served as prisons
and classrooms. In Ireland, hollow trees became hermitages for
medieval monks seeking solitude and penance. In India, fig trees
are an embodiment of the human psyche and a dwelling for the

gods. Around the world, people have revered trees for their commercial value, environmental luster, and visual splendor.

But it is the longevity of trees that tantalizes our senses, piques our curiosity, and engenders myriad often unanswered questions. What conditions lead to their old age? How are they able to survive generations of environmental threats and human interference? Why are some species consistently old, while others topple with the slightest breeze?

In 2016, author and amateur naturalist Fiona Stafford published her well-regarded book *The Long, Long Life of Trees*. In it, Stafford proposes that since the beginnings of history, trees have served humankind in countless ways, but our relationship with trees has many dimensions beyond mere practicality. She argues that trees are so entwined with the breadth of human experience that they are our inspiring and constant companions. Yet, she notes, quite frequently we know very little about these botanical stalwarts.

This book, a quest to understand trees and their longevity, had its genesis in a lofty and spreading copse of camphor trees, blue gum eucalyptus, and California sycamores in the backyard of a ranch house in west Los Angeles in the mid-1950s. The trees were nondescript to the casual observer, but for a young lad with an imagination born of an obsessive reading habit, they became a magnificent Arthurian castle, a rambling frontier fort along the Oregon Trail, a rocket ship speeding toward a soon-to-explode distant world, and a formidable pirate ship.

I had constructed a two-story treehouse made of rescued lumber, discarded timbers, and the castoffs of a nearby construction project. The structure—with separate rooms, an extended balcony, and an ambiance that only a young boy could enjoy—was my solace from the outside world. With Wally, the family dog, as my sidekick, I was an explorer, swashbuckler, adventurer, and captain. These were trees of possibilities as well as discoveries.

During my formative years, my father and I would journey north out of the noisy urban environment that was southern California and into the Mammoth Lakes region of eastern California. There we would ride horses deep into the John Muir Wilderness to fish for golden trout, hike long trails, and commune with a green and vibrant environment. We would traipse through forests of long-needled pines and meander through peaceful woods of white firs that soothed the senses.

Then, when I was thirteen and deemed not working up to my academic potential, my parents enrolled me in the Orme School, a distinguished college preparatory school on a forty-thousand-acre working cattle ranch in the high desert of central Arizona. There towering cottonwood trees abounded along the dry wash of Ash Creek and around the perimeter of the central barnyard. Each fall their leaves turned a golden hue, and when a gentle wind blew the trees shimmered and rustled. In spring their characteristic cotton puffs, which transported seeds long distances, would cloud the air; clinging to clothing, clustering on screen doors, and concealing themselves in the corners of our classrooms. The orbs would sweep across campus and up toward the surrounding mesas in a persistent assertion of nature's renewal and rebirth.

One particular cottonwood tree loomed outside "Old Main," the school's dining hall. Each day students passed by to eat their meals or gather for club meetings. Wind blew through its branches, singing an ancient melody that often found its way inside the building.

In later years I would understand the transformative and cathartic power of forays into untamed lands. At the University of Arizona, history courses and passages into the Coronado National

Forest exposed me to the wisdom of Indigenous people. Here I absorbed the knowledge of trees through the four aspects of personal being: mind, body, emotion, and spirit. In the arc of mountains and the expanse of desert I experienced the personal authority of beings most grand, a concert of education and growth. After graduation, I enlisted in the US Coast Guard and spent four years stationed on Government Island just across the bay from San Francisco. Upon my discharge from the service, my wife, two children, and I moved to Pennsylvania ("Penn's Woods," the only state named for trees) to live in pastoral communities, our rural apartments and rustic houses surrounded by woods that would offer both peace and serenity from the challenges of teaching young people, the demands of a doctoral program, and the rigors of writing.

As I entered the world of academia, my wife and I discovered the rich and varied state parks of the Keystone State. We would pack up the car with nonperishable groceries, a waterproof tent, and other necessary camping tools to seek remote spots amid rugged geographies. Quite often we would pitch our tent inside the security of white pines, eastern hemlocks, or Norway spruces. Our days would find us along mountainous trails or settled in camp chairs with thick books in hand. We spent evenings in the embrace of a campfire beneath a canopy of scented pines. We continue those adventures to this day.

In 2012, champion cyclist and motivational speaker Dan Buettner published a book, *The Blue Zones: 9 Lessons for Living Longer from the People Who've Lived the Longest*, about human longevity. Buettner and his associates identified several areas around the world in which the inhabitants exceeded normal expectations for human life. Significant numbers of people in these regions were living well into their eighties, nineties, and even hundreds. The researchers were able to tease out several fundamental reasons why these people beat the odds to live rich and extended lives. Factors included engaging in activity, limiting calories, having a sense of purpose, relieving stress, placing an emphasis on family, and enjoying a sense of community. Also recommended is a regular glass of wine.

What most struck me in Buettner's book was the fact that a significant percentage of our personal and individual longevity is determined not by a roll of the hereditary dice, but by the choices we make in our lives. That is to say, our decision not to smoke, to limit our intake of red meat, to engage in sustained physical activity, and to participate in communal groups has something significant to say about how long we will live. Scientific research has convincingly demonstrated that human longevity is at least in part something we choose, not always something we unknowingly inherit from an ancestral gene pool.

Yet for the 60,065 species of trees around the world, there is no choice. Their evolution, and thus their longevity, is often a matter of environmental luck or circumstance, including the vagaries of climate, insects, genetics, fire, geography, geology, summer storms, and, of course, time. I wanted to learn more about those factors. However, I approached the quest not as an effort to secure ultimate answers but as an adventure of mind, spirit, and body that might generate questions for which there may be no perfect answers. I also sought to pursue thoughts that might not always be cognitively comfortable but rather pulsated with wonder. I wanted to learn about the extremes of longevity in the natural world as celebrations of the wisdom of nature in preserving and extending life forms that are divergent and different and as wondrous as the arrival of a newborn child or the wedding of your favorite niece. So, too, was I reminded of the admonition of Saint Bernard of Clairvaux (1090–1153): "More things are learnt in the woods than from books. Animals, trees, and rocks teach you things not to be found elsewhere." In truth,

I wanted to solidify my connection and communion with nature. As I was to discover, longevity tells part of the story of some unique botanical specimens that have successfully taken on the best and worst the world has to offer and have survived quite well over the millennia.

The book you hold is an odyssey in the fullest sense of the word. First, it is a compendium of several physical journeys to places both remote and mysterious, stations across the North American continent that harbor distinguished forests or singular trees. Second, it is also an odyssey of the mind, a congeries of intellectual wanderings and personal quests for answers. In both expeditions my desire was to pursue insights, ask deep questions, and ponder the possibilities of an extended life. In my search for enlightenment I journeyed forth, thirsty for firsthand information about species whose evolutionary intelligence was far greater than mine. I wanted to touch ancient trees, visit their habitats, commune with their leafy branches, and spend time in their shade. I also tackled a range of scientific documents, engaged in numerous eye-opening interviews, and pursued a wealth of arboreal books and their authors.

Early in the process, I decided to title this book *In Search of the Old Ones* because it is as much about a personal search for answers as it is about the trees that have "mastered" some of nature's genuine secrets and used them to their own evolutionary advantage. This was not an attempt to find absolute truths, which I will leave to philosophers, but rather to seek some form of illumination along with the generation of more powerful questions. In his essay "The Passing Wisdom of Birds," the naturalist and writer Barry Lopez eloquently urges us "to cultivate within ourselves a sense of mystery—to see that the possibilities for an expression of life in any environment . . . are larger than we can predict or understand, and that is all right."

As I was to discover, the evolution of trees, and thus their longevity, is as much a matter of environmental luck and circumstance as it is of the roll of the dice of climate, predators, genetics, geography, and time. As a writer of science, I am interested not only in how gnarled and windswept trees in a desolate environment have effectively staved off the travails of old age or how an inconspicuous plant can cling to a scrubby hillside in southern California for more than 130 centuries, but also by what leads to these chance occurrences. Nature holds her mysteries close to the breast, and I was determined to examine them via personal visits, vibrant conversations, and extended readings (beneath shady trees, of course). By embarking on this naturalistic journey, I thought I might discover environmental gospels heretofore hidden.

More than fifty thousand years before the ancient pyramids of Egypt rose alongside the Nile, a rich and vibrant ecosystem existed on an expansive shoreline considerably south of modern-day Mobile, Alabama. This was an earlier age, a time when glaciers locked up much of Earth's water and sea levels were up to four hundred feet (122 m) lower than they are today. What are now islands were hills towering several hundred feet above the landscape. The shoreline was between thirty and sixty miles (48–96 km) farther offshore than the present one. The area around Mobile Bay was a vast forested valley split by numerous rivers and streams, a scene not unlike modern-day redwood forests. A diverse assembly of megafauna inhabited this terrestrial expanse: hefty browsers, predatory carnivores, and skittering amphibians roamed throughout.

It was during this era that marching tracts of bald cypress forests spread around the Gulf Coast. But a long series of natural climatic events and rising sea levels killed these trees, burying them under suffocating layers of thick sediment and preserving them for tens of thousands of years. The mud prevented decomposition by cutting off oxygen and creating an anoxic environment, essentially an underwater crypt that entombed the trees for the ages.

In 2004, scientists discovered this ancient cypress forest—positioned eight miles (12.9 km) off the Alabama coast and sixty feet (18.2 m) underwater—in the wake of Hurricane Ivan. According to Ben Raines, one of the early divers at the site, the forest represents a treasure trove of information that provides new insights into everything from regional climate, annual rainfall, and insect populations to the types of plants that inhabited the Gulf Coast long before humans ever trod these environs. Raines further underscored the significance of the site when he noted that the trees discovered in the underwater forest date to an ice age sixty thousand years ago.

Kristine DeLong, an associate professor in the Department of Geography and Anthropology at Louisiana State University, was one of the lead scientists on this underwater discovery. She dove the site in 2013 and recovered numerous samples of the underwater forest. Dating of those samples revealed a forest extant for approximately 42,000 to 74,000 years. I asked her about the scientific significance of the underwater forest. She told me that this was one of the first times scientists had ever found a buried forest so well preserved. She recalled how the wood looked incredibly fresh, and to date it and find out that was more than fifty thousand years old was a surprise.

During our conversation, DeLong reminded me that climate change is not a recent environmental issue; it also refers to previous long-term changes in Earth's climate. One of the things scientists noted was that the recovered trees still had their bark attached, which usually means they were buried quickly rather than over an extended period. Such an event could occur, scientists conjecture, if the Gulf of Mexico experienced a rapid increase in overall sea levels—the result, perhaps, of an accelerated melting of glacial ice. The resultant rise of sea levels, a consequence of an evolutionary increase in global temperatures, would seriously affect the longevity of ice age trees.

So, too, would a similar increase in present-day sea levels affect shoreline inhabitants. For example, in February 2022, a report by the National Oceanic and Atmospheric Administration (NOAA) projected that ocean levels along the US coastline will rise by an average of one foot (0.3 m) by the year 2050. Scientists ascribe this intensification of rising seas to unmitigated greenhouse gas pollution driven primarily by the burning of fossil fuels. As a result, glaciers will melt at a faster rate, worsening the threat of flooding in dozens of highly populated cities. NOAA estimates that residents of the Gulf Coast should anticipate fourteen to eighteen inches (35.5–46 cm) of sea-level rise by 2050; those along the East Coast of the United States should expect a ten- to fourteen-inch (25.4–35.5 cm) rise.

An increase in worldwide temperatures will produce a range of negative effects on earth's climate system as well as its inhabitants. Tens of thousands of years ago, it forced the melting of enormous glaciers with a concomitant rise in sea levels and an inundation of shorelines. Today average global temperatures are also rising at rates previously unknown. Greenhouse gases such as carbon dioxide and methane produced by burning fossil fuels trap heat in Earth's lower atmosphere. The resulting higher temperatures melt permafrost, expand deserts, increase the intensity of storms, exacerbate wildfires, and force glacial retreat. Equally significant is that countless species, both plants and animals, will have to adapt to new ecosystems or face extinction.

That raises an interesting question: Because of climate change, do ancient trees now have an expiration date?

As we examine the long lives of specific species and specific individuals, a whispering voice in the back of our heads may remind us that although the lives of select trees may be long and vibrant, so, too, are they subject to current events, many never yet encountered in their heritage. Not inconsequentially, in September 2022 the Tree Foundation noted that many scientists are vitally concerned that trees, both young and old, are facing an unprecedented level of extinction. They posit that the state of the world's trees has been an ongoing issue for decades now, but ever more rapid climate change is forcing us to face massive issues that could threaten entire ecosystems, including any old trees within them.

The Tree Foundation's concern was underscored in December 2022 when the US Forest Service reported the discovery of 1.1 million acres (445,200 ha) of dead firs in Oregon's forests. This was the most arboreal damage recorded in Oregon in a single season over the preceding seventy-five years. Researchers referred to the blighted landscape as "firmageddon," signifying how a persistent drought, initiated and sustained by rising temperatures, had devastated once verdant hillsides.

Many forests are also moving northward and upward. Rising temperatures associated with the persistent march of climate change across the planet are changing the environmental requisites for many species of trees, often at astonishing rates. Vast territories where trees were once prolific and robust are emptying as trees inch their way across the landscape to seek climes more favorable to their survival. Even the venerable Great Basin bristlecone pines (chapters 1–3) that have established their ancient roots in the hardscrabble substrate of California's White Mountains for more than five thousand years are now migrating up the slopes, "pushed" by higher temperatures that are taking years from their lives. When trees move, their populations decline, even trees that have survived the millennia.

Throughout my decades, I have come to see trees as wise counselors. They have offered some of life's best lessons and necessary respites from an overcrowded schedule or a demanding project. They are my compatriots. I camp under their limbs, study their spread, and travel long distances to view their splendor. I have become an ardent admirer of trees not just for their magnificence but also for their endurance.

Now another arboreal adventure awaits, a journey into new territories and mysterious dominions, and I invite you to join me in my travels across space and time to examine the longevity of selected trees and the lessons that lie in their lives. In this journey, each chapter includes a historical anecdote that places the germination of a particular species in a precise time and place, both in the world at large and at the specific location of the designated forest or tree. Each of these anecdotes, whether fictional or real, comes from historical records and texts. They offer both perspective and insight into times and places long since gone.

These chapters are also sojourns to regions of the United States where old-timers have survived, endured, and lived far beyond human perception. These escapes into mysterious territories of both ecology and contemplation are exercises in admiration as much as they are description. Through them, we will look at life through several lenses—environmental, geographical, anthropological, historical, and biographical, and of course with wonderment.

In the pages that follow, I invite you to position yourself temporarily in the domains of towering redwoods (>2,000 years old), primordial bristlecone pines (5,072+ years old), foreboding bald cypresses (2,628+ years old), a quaking aspen grove (~8,000–12,000 years old), and more. I invite you to stand among organisms that have held their environmental wisdom beyond our experience but within our vision. According to Zach St. George, author of the book *The Journeys of Trees: A Story About Forests, People, and the Future*, what most arouses the inner philosopher in us is not trees' size or shape or ubiquity but their age. As he puts it, there is a good chance any given tree will outlast any given person, and so trees form a bridge beyond the usual human experience, a tangible, living link to the past and perhaps to the future.

I hope that when you close this book at its end you will have discovered insights about select trees and select forests that are at once revealing as well as instructive. I hope you will see ancient trees as compendiums of insightful discoveries and compelling introspection. These organisms may not be within our everyday encounters, but they are our evolutionary partners nonetheless. They may offer us life-changing information we have hitherto been too rushed to see, busy to accept, or reluctant to embrace. And so we may need to experience ancient trees a little differently, a little more deeply, a little more closely.

In every walk with nature one receives far
more than he seeks.—John Muir

I

Part I

Oldest
of the Old

They are indomitable, resolute, and old. Very old. They survive in a brutally hostile environment that readily welcomes no other plant. Their existence is one of extreme temperatures, towering elevations, nutrient-deficient soils, insufficient rainfall, an oxygen-deprived atmosphere, gale-force winds, heavy winter snows, and the constant bombardment of solar energy. Here they stand through long decades, expanded centuries, and an interminable parade of millennia.

Great Basin bristlecone pines (*Pinus longaeva*) are exemplars of longevity. Often cited as the longest-lived trees on the planet, their ages defy expectations and exceed "average" lives. Specimens three thousand and four thousand years old are not uncommon in the high White Mountains of eastern California or the remote slopes of Great Basin National Park in Nevada. Most astounding, lodged in the sanctuary of a hillside deep in the Ancient Bristlecone Pine Forest stands a most patient tree that has lived beyond five thousand years. It is older than old.

These three chapters will introduce some of the most remarkable trees to inhabit the planet, beings extant since before the beginning of the Bronze Age in the Ancient Near East and the initiation of the Late Archaic period in the American Southwest. You will travel through two remarkable forests harboring incredible stalwarts, visit a solitary tree existing at the edge of survival, and journey to a place where perhaps the most egregious act of dendrochronological malfeasance was ever committed. You will discover that ancient trees, particularly old bristlecone pines, have some remarkable stories to share.

These three chapters are tales of endurance and tales of permanence. They are celebrations of a long-lived species that has successfully endured conditions that would fell lesser plants—with one notable exception. They have turned environmental adversity to their evolutionary advantage. Spread across forbidding terrain, these trees continue to reach for the sky at altitudes more than two miles (3.2 km) above sea level. So, too, do they reach the outer limits of longevity—a true "survival of the fittest."

CHAPTER 1

Old Warriors

Common name: Great Basin bristlecone pine
Scientific binomial: *Pinus longaeva*
Age: 4,000–5,000+ years
Location: White Mountains, California,
Ancient Bristlecone Pine Forest

2985 BCE, Outside Sippar, 32.4 Miles (60 km) North of Babylon
The wind was ever-present, spiraling across the landscape and coating fields, wagons, huts, cattle, and humans with thin shadows of dust. Swirls and eddies swept through desiccated valleys and over barren hillsides, gathering a billion particles in their journeys. Doors and windows were of little consequence, for the dust always found a thin crack or narrow passage to infiltrate interiors with successive layers of the surrounding geology.

Enlil-zi-shagal squatted in the midafternoon sun, wiping his brow with the back of his hand while simultaneously sweeping the small cloud of flies away from his face. Before him on the ground lay a thin mat of carefully woven vegetation from the nearby Euphrates River. A master potter, he formed his clay masterpieces on this mat; his creations often fetched many handfuls of barley, particularly during Akitu, the festival that took place during the first full moon after the spring equinox, marking the new year. He had learned the craft from his father, a hereditary transmittal of knowledge that preserved both tradition and honor. He would pass that heritage to his firstborn son, who would in turn ensure that the artistry of the family elders would be maintained and celebrated for another generation.

It was also during this time that the *Epic of Gilgamesh* came into being. Scribed on twelve clay tablets, it tells of the King of Uruk, his friend Enkidu, and their journey to the sacred Cedar Forest ("On the third day they drew near to the Lebanon"). There they engage Humbaba, Guardian of the Cedar Forest, in a fierce battle. In the aftermath, the two friends cut down all the trees to construct a large raft and eventually a great cedar gate for the city of Nippur. This Mesopotamian myth established the Cedars of Lebanon as perhaps the most famous trees in all of antiquity.

Myths aside, the potters of Mesopotamia, such as Enlil-zi-shagal, used woven mats to turn their vessels under construction as they added coils of clay. When one part of the vessel had been formed, the potter would turn the mat one-quarter to the right and continue the spiral, the artistry of his hands lending symmetry to each creation.

From over Enlil-zi-shagal's shoulder, the eldest son, Ilu-asu, often watched, diligently analyzing the lay of hands, the tilt of fingers, and the coordination of actions. He never asked questions, for his role was to observe. This trade passed down through generations not by words or diagrams, but more by actions and insights. It was a talent best learned through observation and contemplation rather than by overt direction.

Between tending the family's small herd of goats, irrigating the plot of vegetables inside the short wall that encircled their house, and performing other chores, twelve-year-old Ilu-asu would occasionally practice his father's art. His initial creations, as for any novice, were irregular, uninspired, and clumsy. Maintaining concentric circles for a well-formed pot was a constant challenge for the young potter. But Ilu-asu persisted, frustrated at having to turn the mat in quarter-circles after adding a section of coil. "There must be a better way," he thought.

Some ingenious artisan had invented that better way a little more than a hundred years earlier: the potter's wheel. But technology moved slowly, and it would be many years before the new invention would reach the dusty Mesopotamian village.

2985 BCE, Eastern California
While Enlil-zi-shagal was creating his masterpieces, another event, seemingly insignificant and assuredly unnoticed, took place some 7,675 miles (12,352 km) to the west. It was in a mountainous region of barren land in what is now eastern California. Once under leagues of an ancient sea, a subduction zone formed at the edge of the North American continent, pulling the earth underneath it and forcing a massive uplift less than five million years ago. The result was the creation of the Sierra Nevada batholith. Since covered with a thick layer of parched substrate, the barren landscape is both expansive and unending. A vast talus field of radiant white soil blankets the ground in all directions. Here, the soil is stark and barren. The thin, rocky substrate, known as dolomite, is a light-colored rock and soil that is predominantly alkaline (a pH higher than 7.0), high in calcium and magnesium and low in phosphorus.

Somehow a seed, likely transported by wind or an animal, lodged in this formidable soil. It secured a favorable purchase beneath a thin layer of dolomite. With just the right quantity of moisture and sunlight, the seed began a botanical journey ingrained in its genetic code, one followed by countless ancestors and descendants. The seed would germinate in the spring, when warm temperatures energized enzymes that broke down the nutritive tissue inside the seed cavity. A primordial root then grew through the splitting seed coat and revealed itself to a world full of sunlight. Photosynthesis was now possible, and the new seedling began making its own nutrients. A long life lay ahead.

Present Day

The sky, resplendent as a shard of Navajo turquoise, highlighted the snow-draped peaks of the Sierra Nevada range. A sea of green needles and twisted limbs flanked me. I had paused on the crest of a sinuous mountain trail surrounded by most ancient beings, gnarled botanical sentinels clinging to a hillside of crumbled dolomite and scree. Birds were absent, as though they were foreigners in a land of limited biology and rugged extremes. But the trees got my attention, evolutionary stalwarts braced against the bitter harshness of this ecosystem and resilient in the face of severe environmental odds.

I had come to the White Mountains of eastern California, specifically the Ancient Bristlecone Pine Forest, to seek counsel with some of the oldest living beings on the planet. I was here to commune with *Pinus longaeva*, trees that have been growing steadily on these seemingly barren mountain tops ever since the development of writing in Sumer and Egypt (~2600 BCE), the beginnings of Stonehenge in what is now England (2400–2200 BCE), and the emergence of the Bronze Age in Crete (3200 BCE). Moreover, many of these same trees were well established centuries before the construction of the Great Pyramid of Giza, the introduction of rice into Malaysia, or the rise to power of the First Dynasty of Ur.

For thousands of years, most of the trees around me have been holding fast to their mountain domain, having established their botanical dominance while early human civilizations were ascending or declining in far distant lands. Indeed, as we will see, bristlecone wood has recorded Earth's history more faithfully than any ancient Roman scribe or modern-day Twitter fanatic. They are illuminators of ancient history; open records of climate, geology, and botany; and whorled pages of data etched into ageless timber and sunburned snags. Mark A. Schlenz, a writer who has spent much time in this ancient forest, makes the point that bristlecone pines often grow in habitats utterly hostile to most other forms of plant life. He writes in *A Day in the Ancient Bristlecone Pine Forest* that these indomitable trees exist where it seems no trees could withstand the harsh environmental conditions of altitude, desert dryness, icy winds, heavy snows, freezing temperatures, infertile soils, and extreme solar exposure.

Great Basin bristlecone pines (*Pinus longaeva*), our focus in this chapter, are one of a trio of long-lived pines that inhabit the American West. They can be found primarily in eastern California, eastern Nevada, and throughout Colorado's western slope. They are famously regarded as the oldest trees in the world. Their two cousins, though less-known, are also long-lived (but not as long as *Pinus longaeva*). These include Rocky Mountain bristlecone pines (*Pinus aristata*), located in Colorado and northern New Mexico, and foxtail pines (*Pinus balfouriana*), which inhabit central and northern California.

Earlier that morning I had departed Big Pine, California, a town of just 1,875 inhabitants cradled in the arid Owens Valley and wedged between the Sierra Nevada and the White Mountains. A distant string of sawtooth peaks, embraced by a searing sky, bordered US 395 to my left. Scattered across their elevation were random pockets of dirty snow lodged in zigzagging ravines carved out by probing sunlight.

US 395 slips through the north end of town and past hardscrabble plants hugging both sides of the road. The road was well baked on this early June morning as I made a right turn to begin my ascent through the foothills up State Route 168, a former mining-era toll road that climbs its way up to 7,313 feet (2,229 m) above sea level, leading to a scrubby plateau known as Cedar Flat.

The road often doubles back on itself in sharp curves, arching loops, and switchbacks like an enormous serpent, writhing and twisting. It commands attention and a quick response on the brake pedal as I approached blind curves and sharp grades around twisting bends.

Eventually I reached the top of the pass and made a left turn onto the ten-mile (16 km) paved road that roves up the mountain face to an oxygen-sucking ten thousand feet (3,048 m) and higher still. Allow me to elaborate: the percentage of the atmosphere composed of oxygen at sea level is 20.9 percent. At an altitude of ten thousand feet, it decreases to 14.3 percent. This significantly reduces the oxygen content of each breath, as well as O_2 saturation in the blood of unacclimatized individuals, like certain writers.

The road loops across the prehistoric face of the mountain, guiding me northward in an exhibition of twists, turns, and altitudinal ascents. I now traveled between random stands of scrub and short trees clustered about the road and sweeping along the hillocks and outcroppings that defined the boundaries of my journey.

The last three miles (4.8 km) to the park entrance winds through isolated clusters of bristlecone pines. Ancient sentinels, they stand against the sky. Biological and evolutionary marvels, bristlecones have laid claim to this mountainside for thousands of years and will continue to do so as long as the climate will allow them to.

Although bristlecone pines have hugged these slopes for thousands of years, their age was not known until 1953 after a fortuitous discovery by dendrochronologist Edmund Schulman. Schulman and a colleague, Frits Went, were doing research in Sun Valley, Idaho, when they came upon a limber pine (*Pinus flexilis*), an ancient tree about 1,650 years old. They realized that there might be more ancient trees awaiting discovery in these mountains. On their way back to Pasadena, California, they decided to make a detour and drive up into the White Mountains to check out a rumor that several very old trees inhabited the high altitudes there. Shortly after their arrival, they located a bristlecone pine tree that a local ranger had named "Patriarch." Samples taken from the tree proved it to be only 1,500 years old. While that wasn't as old as they hoped, it planted a mental seed: the possibility that they might find considerably older trees in the high country.

Born in 1908, Edmund Schulman grew up in Brooklyn, eventually moving to Arizona. In 1932 Andrew E. Douglass, an astronomer at the University of Arizona, hired Shulman as an assistant. Douglass was studying the relationship between sunspot cycles and climate change through an analysis of tree rings. Douglass had used tree rings to determine the age of the Pueblo Bonito settlement in the Ancestral Puebloan ceremonial complex at Chaco Canyon, New Mexico, a discovery that helped to rewrite the history of the ancient Southwest. That research was pivotal in Douglass's securing funding to establish the Laboratory of Tree-Ring Research at the university in 1937.

Schulman earned a post as an assistant astronomer at the Steward Observatory. Later he took over as editor of *Tree-Ring Bulletin*. In 1945 he became a full-time faculty member and assumed his duties in the Laboratory of Tree-Ring Research. Schulman's work there convinced him that he needed to return to the White Mountains, which he and his assistant C. W. Ferguson did in 1954 and 1955. They discovered that the oldest trees in this singular landscape lived in some of the most extreme conditions, typically at elevations above ten thousand feet. Most amazing was that these trees were growing in such inhospitable locales marked by lack of viable soil, extreme fluctuations in temperature, and scant moisture.

During the course of his investigations, Schulman took numerous core samples from specimens throughout this high-altitude enclave. It was then that he ventured into a grove of bristlecones near what is now his namesake, the Schulman Grove. He took a core sample from one of the gnarly trees and headed back to his camp to begin counting the annual growth rings. He counted, counted, and counted. Finally finishing in the dark of night, he counted rings beyond the year 2046 BCE. Imagine his amazement and exuberance when he realized he had discovered the first tree in the world known to exceed four thousand years in age—and it was still living. It was a scientific breakthrough of incalculable importance. Schulman named the tree "Pine Alpha."

As it turned out, Schulman's four-thousand-year-old tree was one of many discoveries he was to make in this area. Additional research over the years revealed scores of trees in this particular grove in the three-thousand- to four-thousand-year-old range. As many as nineteen individual trees in the Ancient Bristlecone Pine Forest exceed four thousand years of age. That is to say, nineteen trees, all still living today, germinated during the time when the Middle Kingdom began in Egypt (~2040 BCE) and at about the same time the Sumerian culture in Mesopotamia ended (~2000 BCE).

In 1957 Schulman returned to the White Mountains to sample additional trees. There he found a tree he affectionately named Methuselah, after the biblical figure who reportedly lived to be 969 years old. He estimated the tree's true age to be near 4,600 years old. As a result, he pronounced Methuselah the "world's oldest known living thing." Subsequent coring and analysis of Methuselah by Tom Harlan at the Laboratory of

Tree-Ring Research dated the innermost tree ring to 2491 BCE. Thus, in 2023 Methuselah's age would be 4,514 years old. Just before his death, Schulman declared, "The capacity of these trees to live so fantastically long may, when we come to understand it fully, perhaps serve as a guidepost on the road to the understanding of longevity in general."

Since its authentication as an old-timer, Methuselah continues to thrive along the 4.5-mile (7.2 km) Methuselah Trail in the Ancient Bristlecone Pine Forest. The tree is currently over fifty feet (15.25 m) tall and still sports healthy foliage and seed cones. It grows at an elevation just shy of ten thousand feet. For a number of years the Forest Service identified the tree with a prominent sign. However, in order to foil vandals and others prone to picking off various souvenir pieces from historical or scientific objects, its exact location has now become a carefully guarded secret. Ask one of the rangers at the visitor's center where Methuselah is located and they will smile and most likely tell you, "Look carefully as you walk along the trail, and you will know you've seen it by the time you return."

Perhaps even more amazing than Methuselah is another as yet unnamed tree that still inhabits this forest. In the late 1950s Schulman cored a certain tree there, but he never had a chance to date it before he died. Tom Harlan worked up the core long after Schulman's passing. As of the growing season of 2023, this tree is 5,073 years old. It would have germinated around 3050 BCE—the time when humans first began to develop a writing system, known as cuneiform script, when the Early Dynastic (Archaic) period started in ancient Egypt, and when the peoples of what is now the Southwest first began to grow corn. This tree is officially the oldest nonclonal tree in the world. (A clonal tree is a plant able to reproduce itself through a process known as vegetative cloning. A clonal tree descends from and is genetically similar to a single common ancestor. Theoretically, a clonal plant can continue propagating itself for hundreds or thousands of years.) This tree's location is another closely guarded secret.

Equally astounding as the age of these living trees is the fact that dead bristlecone pine wood also offers scientific clues about past millennia earlier than any of the living ancients in the forest. That's because bristlecone wood that has died and fallen to the ground can remain virtually intact for thousands of years in the harsh, cold, and arid environment of these mountains. As a result, a tree's growth rings can preserve a record of past weather patterns, climatic conditions, environmental changes, volcanic eruptions, fires, and even floods. By finding overlaps in the tree ring patterns of living bristlecones and those in fallen wood from long-dead trees, scientists have been able to identify climactic and environmental events going back to the last ice age, thus establishing a continuous chronology of environmental events for approximately eleven thousand years.

Even more remarkable is the fact that bristlecone tree rings have rewritten history. For example, in the 1960s archaeologists dated the origins of European civilization by measuring the radioactive decay of carbon isotopes in ancient artifacts. What they failed to do, however, was adjust those calculations for periodic changes in Earth's atmospheric carbon levels. The wood from bristlecone pines provided samples that scientists could date precisely. Those scientists dated bristlecone samples by counting their growth rings; they then measured the amount of carbon-14 (C-14) in those same samples. They discovered that the radiocarbon dating process was providing dates that were too young. As a result, scientists painstakingly established a calibration factor to correct the previous dating process.

Scientists then reexamined and amended faulty C-14 data obtained before the bristlecone pine calibration. Archaeologists subsequently found that some artifacts discovered in Europe were actually one thousand years or more older than previously thought. This revision of archaeological site dates led historians to a reinterpretation of cultural diffusion throughout the Mediterranean and across Europe.

With the bristlecone pine and scientific dating methods, we have a tool that allows us to look backward for approximately one hundred centuries to a time when the world's total population was a mere five million people (it is now just over eight billion), a time when the first bladed tools were developed, and to a time when woolly mammoths, saber-toothed cats, and giant ground sloths wandered North America, the end of the Upper Paleolithic or Late Stone Age.

Dendrochronology, as we saw in the preface, is the science of tree-ring dating based on an analysis of patterns of tree rings, also known as growth rings. Dendrochronologists can accurately date the time at which a tree forms each of its growth rings, often to the exact calendar year. This is because under normal conditions, a tree will grow one ring for each year of its life. In extreme circumstances, such as a pronounced drought, rings may be extremely thin or sometimes nonexistent. Devastating forest fires can also affect the appearance of rings. The newest rings will be those closest to the bark, while the oldest rings will be those closest to the center of the tree.

Scientists at the Laboratory of Tree-Ring Research at the University of Arizona use a method of tree ring dating known as "cross-dating by skeleton plotting." With this method, scientists take several core samples from a homogeneous area or an area of similar environmental conditions. They then match up the growth-ring characteristics of those various samples,

one on top of the other, to determine the exact year of formation
for each ring. Scientists cross-date the rings by marking a
tree's ring width variation on graph paper strips, or the
"skeleton plot."

Tree rings often reflect climatic conditions. Lots of moisture and a long growing season often result in a wide tree ring.
Drought conditions and a shorter growing season produce a
thinner ring. Analysis of the width of tree rings in a single tree
can thus reveal the climatic conditions in a specific area over
long periods of time. Researchers then match similar patterns of
variation in individual plots (representing individual trees)
among trees.

Valerie Trouet, a dendroclimatologist at the Laboratory of
Tree-Ring Research, told me that dendrochronology is in a unique
position to reveal the interactions between human history and
environmental science because it "sits right at the nexus of ecology, climatology, and human history." She studies wood, but she
also studies the history of climate—for example, how climate has
influenced fire history, how it has influenced the rise and fall of
past civilizations, and how have we humans influenced the climate, especially in the Anthropocene of our here and now, where
humans are changing the climate. How will that climate change
influence ecosystems and influence our human systems? Dendrochronologists are on the case.

After exiting my car near the Ancient Bristlecone Pine Forest visitor
center, I slung my backpack over my shoulders, took a long gulp of
water, and gazed up at the mountain before me. The summer sun
suffused the landscape with a vibrancy that highlighted even the
minutest of botanical features on the hundreds of trees before me.

Approaching the ascending geography from the parking area, I began my trek on the Discovery Trail, a one-mile (1.6 km) labyrinthine walk whose first half meanders up some three hundred feet (91 m) in elevation while crossing the mountain face. Well named, it passes by many of the original bristlecone pine discoveries Schulman made in the 1950s.

At this elevation the bristlecones dominated, a kingdom of arboreal majesty and extended lives. Typically, Great Basin bristlecone pines occur at elevations from about 7,200 feet (2,195 m) to 12,000 feet (3,658 m) above sea level, and here was a sweet spot for the species. Indeed, about fifty yards (45.75 m) up the dusty, rock-strewn trail, I came upon the hardened remains of a toppled ancient, a bristlecone pine dated at more than 3,200 years when it died. While its age is immediately astounding, most significant is the fact that this particular specimen died in approximately 1676 CE. Its birthday, then, was approximately 1524 BCE, near the end of the fifteenth dynasty in Egypt, when early traces of the Maya civilization began in Belize, and when the Phoenicians first developed an alphabet. Approaching the tree, I closely examined some of the exposed limbs and roots, noting that a substantial number of the annual tree rings were packed extremely close together. I would later learn that in many bristlecones more than one hundred years of tree rings can be found in a mere one inch of growth. Obviously, this suggests that severe drought conditions are a persistent way of life here rather than a random climatic anomaly.

I slowly rubbed my hands over the weathered exterior of the tree, captivated by its history and marveling at its endurance. Massive, hardened, and rough, this wood will eventually decompose with time, but its ruggedness suggests the elements will have a fierce battle breaking it down, slow molecule by very slow molecule.

Quite often bristlecone pines will have exposed roots, revealing the constant downward slide of a mountainside.

After paying my respects, I continued my expedition upward. My feet kicked up small clouds of dust as I clambered along the ascending path. My pace slowed with the altitude. I couldn't help but think how these trees have endured for eons and, while many are standing robust and vibrant, scores have fallen, their remains strewn across the ground. Although they are no longer living, these historical recorders are silent reminders of what Earth was like long before humans ever set foot near these environs.

I paused to stand beside another ancient, a botanical incongruity whose wood was seemingly dead—knurled, twisted, dry, and without apparent signs of life, yet there were hardy bunches of needles and rich tufts of green clinging to the ends. As I took in the magnificence of this specimen, I noted a coal-black varnish on several portions of the branches and trunk, which could be a sign of a disease or sunburn. Its scorched appearance reminded me of an overdone porterhouse steak. Yet the tree was surviving, doggedly clinging to life, even though more than half of it appeared to be dead. Then its roots, shallow and exposed, captured my attention. Most of a bristlecone's roots grow close to the surface of the soil to seize the scarce moisture that falls on these mountains. Bristlecone roots grow primarily in the spring, when the snow has melted and the soil has warmed, and then again in the fall if there is sufficient moisture. In rocky terrain, roots wrap tightly around boulders, forming a strong anchorage, and they seek water in minute cracks and miniscule rivulets. There is usually no taproot. Instead, lateral mother roots leave the trunk like the arms of an enormous octopus, extending as far as fifty feet (15.25 m) from the trunk. Almost everywhere I looked, I could easily see serpentine roots that had surfaced on slopes where constant erosion had exposed them.

Soil erosion is a persistent consequence of mountain living. Water and ice are the primary agents of topographic change, but gravity is also at work, slowly but steadily dragging down the mountains. As I looked around, it became evident that the exposed roots of many trees showed the effects of thousands of years of steadfast and resolute erosion. On a nearby tree, I noted the original soil line on the roots. I also noticed that nearly three feet (0.9 m) of soil had washed or blown away at its southward-facing side, thus exposing much of the main root system to the elements. Soil loss on one side of a slope-hugging tree can eventually destabilize it, causing it to crash to the ground. However, this particular tree's roots had caught a grand cache of massive boulders on its uphill side, thus creating a gravitational standoff. It may well stand for a few more centuries.

Interestingly, the gravitational slide of soil and rocks is both constant and measurable, and the average rate of erosion in these mountains is approximately one foot (0.3 m) of soil loss per thousand years. As a result, some scientists have used this information to estimate the ages of ancient trees simply by measuring the exact amount of erosion. I decided to do my own rough estimation of this tree's age using the length of my hand, which I know to be eight inches (20.3 cm), as my measuring tool. Bracing myself on the hillside, I found the prominent ring around the original base of the tree. Positioning my hands, one after the other, down the southward side of the tree, I measured a total of 5.5 hands, or roughly forty-four inches (1.1 m). Thus, by my rudimentary calculations, this old-timer was approaching four thousand years in age.

While exposed roots are an inevitability of alpine life, they are also a liability. The exposure subjects a tree to a host of life-threatening diseases and insect infestation. Fungus, rot, and several parasitic creatures swoop in and attack the tree's new vulnerability and often have a negative effect on its longevity. Some arborists have postulated root exposure as the leading cause of mortality for these ancient trees.

A few more steps, a few more turns, and a few more feet in elevation and I was on a narrow ledge at the summit of Discovery Trail. Gathering in the sights, I rested on an old log that lay parallel to the trail, taking in the magnificence of this ancient vista. A ridge of snowcapped mountains rambled off to my right, while tawny expanses of rolling scrub fanned out far below me. The air was crisp and vibrant, while all around were patient oldsters: stands of trees here long before Polynesians crossed the Pacific Ocean to discover the Hawaiian Islands (1219–1266 CE), long before the birth of Christ (~6–4 BCE), and long before much of the ancient history I studied in school ever took place.

That bristlecones are able to survive on the seeming barrenness of these mountains is ultimately dependent on two significant environmental factors. First of all, dolomite is light-colored, which means it reflects considerably more light than would the humus of lower-elevation gardens. As a result, the substrate is cooler. This lower temperature tends to favor the specific germination of bristlecone seeds (more on this later). For bristlecone pines, as it is for several varieties of plant life, the ambient temperature of the soil affects the germination rate. In essence, each plant has its own preferred soil warmth. Bristlecones "prefer" cool.

There is another, equally significant, factor that favors dolomite, especially for bristlecones. Dolomite soils have a higher total water storage capacity than many other soils. As a result, the increased level of moisture retention enhances the overall germination rate of bristlecone seeds while also providing reserves of water during long periods of drought.

I traversed an arid and parched landscape virtually devoid of significant moisture. Indeed, the White Mountains experience an average annual precipitation rate of only 12.9 inches (32.8 cm). One of the bristlecone's most distinctive characteristics is its tolerance to drought. Not only do its branched, shallow roots maximize water absorption, but its waxy needles and thick needle cuticles also aid in water retention. Most pine trees regrow their needles every four to six years. Bristlecones can retain their needles for thirty-five or more years, and these old needles remain fully functional throughout that time. In fact, nearly four-decade-old bristlecone needles are still able to regulate water loss and photosynthesize. As a result, the tree saves considerable and vital energy.

This singular landscape also imparts a vital lesson in competition. The seeming infertility of the soil precluded other foreign vegetation from competing for the same space and nutrients necessary to bristlecones. Indeed, fertile soil, a commandment of serious gardeners, tends to breed more competition and more plant species seeking a place in an ecosystem. Conversely, a predominantly infertile landscape often leads to considerably less competition among the species that can tolerate it. Most plants cannot tolerate the highly alkaline dolomite soil, but bristlecone pines endure it well. For the most part, they exist unchallenged.

In stark contrast to the world below, a world punctuated by the cacophony of loud music, construction sounds, boisterous factories, rumbling diesels, supersonic disturbances, and the penetrating intrusions of urban noise, there is a distinct peacefulness here, a serenity that envelopes human wanderers as much as it does the trees. I noted that these trees also inhabit a landscape well beyond the onslaught of the "civilized" world.

Rested and reflective, I shouldered my backpack and traversed the last half-mile (0.8 km) of the trail. On my downward descent, I wound my way through small packets of trees grasping the hillside. In between these patches were massive accumulations of vermillion-shaded rocks scattered across the landscape. This rough-hewn rubble is quartzite, metamorphically melted sandstone unhurriedly fragmented by the erosional forces of wind, rain, and ice as the mountains rose from their aquatic past and inched toward the sky in a geological transformation eons in the making. Its shades of pink and red are due to varying amounts of iron oxide, the main component of rust, as well as other mineral impurities.

This part of my journey complete, I sat at a picnic table, consumed my lunch, and contemplated my presence here. In some ways I was just a brief organic speck, a miniscule interloper among these timeless giants, which had endured generations of environmental challenges and were still living their lives. As ever, resilient.

Later that day, when the sun radiated both brilliance and heat, I set out on the 4.5-mile (7.25 km) Methuselah Trail, which lopes through broad vistas and widening groves of bristlecones across a hilly terrain behind the visitor center. The initial passage was steep, and I could feel the tingling effects of altitude sickness: a slight pulsing in my head and a labored breath. After less than a mile, I rested beside a dignified and ancient tree. Reverently touching its bark, I felt a dry, weather-beaten exterior much like timeworn shingles on an old house. The texture was rough and gritty, revealing multiple centuries of environmental onslaught. Short green sprouts emerged from its crown, a sign of continued life even though about 95 percent of the tree was dead. Spindly and naked branches, a spiky, empty top, and bare wood on limbs and exposed roots are testament to its endurance.

Tree after tree along my path evidenced a curiously high proportion of dead trunk and branch wood. It often appeared as though a great majority of a single tree was composed of parched and lifeless trunks, a twisted and tangled display of exposed roots, and an environmental solemnity frequently characteristic of lifeless organisms. Yet most of these trees were striated with thin bands of living root and stem tissue, conduits that allow them to get essential nutrients and life-affirming water out to the sparse foliage that festoons a few low-lying branches or crowns a mostly denuded trunk.

Farther along the trail, I stop beside two trees standing side by side. One is most certainly dead, an ancient and gnarled snag with empty limbs and an absence of bark. The other is still living, its branches festooned with rich clumps of emerald needles. The dead one is twisted and knotted, with knobby, spindly arms sticking out in myriad directions. Its partner, the living one, cants slightly to the left. It has retained about 15 percent of its pine needles on the ends of assorted branches. Both stand proud on this mountain, as they have for eons. Who knows, perhaps they sprouted together some two to three thousand years ago. Both have weathered decades of travails and centuries of storms. One has succumbed to the ravages of time, the other clings precariously to life. Yet they are still bonded to each other, partners against the forces of nature.

After additional hydration and hundreds of steps down a short canyon, I found myself stopping along the trail to photograph another tree. Like several of its neighbors in this expanse, the tree pulses with life. Running my fingers over the bristles, I discovered them to be soft and seemingly full of energy and vigor—features emblematic of pines growing at much lower elevations. This young tree was perhaps only a few centuries old, getting a foothold on a life that will extend far past every person who now occupies the planet.

Bristlecone pines do not age rapidly. One researcher reported consistent average heights of approximately six inches (15.25 cm) for forty-year-old "seedlings." Additional research estimates the diameter growth rate of many bristlecones at about one inch per century. Mature trees in harsh sites often cease to grow taller after reaching fifteen to thirty feet (4.5–9 m). In 1998, researchers looked at some of the factors that might affect bristlecone aging and discovered that the concept of senescence, or the condition and process of deterioration with age, including a loss of a cell's power of division and growth, may not apply to these trees. What often results are tiny amounts of new growth each year. But that growth is particularly significant in that the wood is hard, resin-filled, and extremely resistant to pine-killing bark beetles, mold, fungus, and decay. In short, although bristlecones may indicate several outward signs of aging, they are still vibrant, living beings. Aging in *Pinus longaeva* is in many ways an act of defiance.

The trail angles and bends, ascends and descends, dips and curves. Its meandering path resembles the bristlecone's tortuous shapes, its branches contorted and distorted, limbs twisted, roots bent, and trunks warped into swirled masses of timber, the result of centuries of blasting winds, arid growing conditions, wild variations in available moisture, and nutrient availability.

For the next hour or so, I transported myself through magnificent views and the ethereal company of these mysterious friends. I passed across hillsides crowded with ancient companions, each one clinging to the soil with both tenacity and determination. Thousands of years of exposure to wind-whipped sand and denuding ice blasts have carved and stunted them. They have prospered where few other plants could ever exist. They are survivors of the first order.

And for Great Basin bristlecone pines, time is not their enemy. It is their companion.

Realm of the Old Man

Common name: Great Basin bristlecone pine

Scientific binomial: *Pinus longaeva*

Age: ~1,500 years

Location: White Mountains, Ancient Bristlecone Pine Forest, California

522 CE, North China, Shanxi Province—North Wei Dynasty

Hui Yin crouched in the corner of her compact earthen hut. The structure, 10 feet (3.05 m) on each side, was but a single room excavated into the side of a small hill. The members of her family—her husband, their two daughters, and her mother—inhabited the sparse dwelling. They cooked outside, and their meals were typical of the time: venison, rice, apricots, edible roots, chestnuts, rabbits, and carp from nearby rivers.

The mountains all around were well-forested with a rich variety of tree species. Those on the more humid north-facing slopes included hazels, ash, maples, and lindens. The drier south-facing mountain slopes featured pines, honey locusts, oaks, and buckthorns. Over several centuries, the extensive natural forests succumbed to the need for cultivated land to provide crops for the growing population. Today, forests cover only about one-fifth of the province.

Hui Yin met her husband, Nian Zhen, at a communal celebration when they were both thirteen. It was clear to village elders that theirs would be a long and fruitful relationship. They married when Hui Yin was sixteen, and all the local and neighboring villagers attended their wedding.

However, one spring when the rivers were harsh and formidable, a flash flood swept Nian Zhen away. Searchers recovered his body downstream and transported it to the village's communal area. Hui Lin wept openly, and the pall cast over the village persisted for many days. Finally, it was the day of the burial. Making sure her metal wedding band was secured on her left ring finger, Hui Lin dressed in a plain gown. Squatting on the dirt floor of the hut, she plunged a knife into her heart.

Knowing the deep and intense love shared by this couple, their family members placed them in the same grave facing each other, laying Hui Lin's head against the left shoulder of her husband and wrapping their arms around each other's waists. Carefully and reverently, villagers covered their bodies with earth and stones. The ceremony that followed celebrated their eternal love with solemn dances and the slow beat of drums. Husband and wife lay together, embracing each other for their journey into the afterlife. It was the ultimate expression of their love.

Fifteen hundred years later, the skeletons of an adult male and an adult female were discovered in a joint burial in Shanxi Province. As a research study published in the *International Journal of Osteoarchaeology* in June 2021 reported, scientists found them in a loving embrace. On the left ring finger of the female was a metal band.

522 CE, Eastern California

At the time of the burial in Shanxi Province, in a territory 6,164 miles (9,914 km) to the east, a young sprout had secured itself in a rugged sea of dolomite. Dolomite, as we saw in chapter 1, is a

primordial substance, made up of small particles of dead organisms, sand, and silt that settled on the bottom of a prehistoric ocean, forming sedimentary deposits some 650 million years ago. Around 350 million years ago, a long and complicated series of geological events began. Major collisions of the Pacific and North American tectonic plates folded, faulted, and uplifted this ocean bottom from below sea level to above ten thousand feet (3,048 m). Mountains formed all around. Indeed, the chalky dolomite that predominates is what gives this region its name: the White Mountains.

Archaeologists have been able to determine that Native Americans occupied these barren mountains for more than ten thousand years. The first physical evidence of their occupation was the discovery of several rock blinds distributed across the topography. These austere shelters date to at least 2500 BCE, when hunters used them while searching out mountain sheep and deer. In later years, Indigenous peoples stored their seed harvests in various camps scattered throughout these rugged mountains.

Expansive fields of glaring substrate highlight the wide, barren land. Aside from occasional accumulations of young trees, the varied vegetation common at lower elevations is scant. Random chips of dead wood punctuate adjacent rocks and crevices. The deep greens of the living trees that cling to this topography stand in sharp contrast to the eye-blazing glare of white earth all around.

But the sprout endures. Staving off the trials and tribulations of this severe ecosystem, it slowly grows, centimeter by centimeter. Throughout the centuries it will survive one of nature's most challenging environments.

Present Day
During my initial sojourn in the Ancient Bristlecone Pine Forest described in the preceding chapter, I took a long morning and

headed to another part of this singular national forest, the Patriarch Grove, a parched landscape twelve miles (19.3 km) north of the park's visitor center, but centuries away in time.

The Grove is at the terminus of a bumpy, twisting, and rocky track that limited my rental car to a top speed of 20 miles per hour (32 km/h). I fixed my attention on the road, gripping the steering wheel for a bone-jarring, forty-minute drive to the uppermost extreme of the timberline. This high altitude of 11,200 feet (3,414 m), with its sparse vegetation, could serve as a backdrop for any number of science fiction movies set on distant planets.

I arrived at a natural amphitheater offering spectacular and scenic views in every direction. Splendid mountains marched off to my left to a vanishing point hundreds of miles in the distance. The crisp edge of an indigo horizon sealed the sky, accentuating the landscape. And, although it was June, a broad patch of clear-white snow still clung to the side of an adjacent hill. It is in that setting that the imposing Patriarch Tree, the world's largest bristlecone pine, stands, germinating at about the time Nian Zhen and Hui Lin died.

Although it is a mere forty-one feet (12.5 m) tall, the Patriarch Tree is a massive specimen, with a fluted, multiple trunk consisting of six major trunks and three smaller ones, thirty-six feet (11 m) in circumference. Most of the trunks have an upright posture, while others, bent by centuries of winds and snow, lean in anomalous and sundry directions. A ragged cluster of smaller and considerably younger trees ring the tree, as though arranged in stilled reverence to this majestic giant, courtiers admiring their king.

Standing before this giant, I observed that soil erosion had exposed much of the base, a conglomeration of major and minor roots. This constant weathering over the years may be responsible for the permanent fusing of these lifelines, forming a braided assembly of alternating dead and living tissue. A rich assembly of bristling green branches shrouded the upper two-thirds of the tree, a supreme emerald crown.

The Patriarch Tree is an emblem of the ages, standing resplendent and grand, its exterior highlighted by a sculptor's assembly of arcing branches in concert with a profusion of verdant needles against a boundless sky. The photos I took barely do it justice, yet this single tree was truly worth the trip, an arboreal sculpture that ranks alongside the best works of the human artistic imagination.

I slowly walked around this sovereign, taking in the extent of its being. Halfway through my transit, I stopped. I paused, listening for other signs of life, other evidence of nature's familiar vibrancy. However, there was nothing. I was alone—without songbirds, the buzz of insects, the sounds of another soul. Silence surrounded this stark, stilled place. The Patriarch Tree stands mute as it has for fifteen centuries and with luck will do so for fifteen more.

The Patriarch Tree first came to public attention through Edmund Schulman's 1958 *National Geographic* article. Since then it has been famously known as the largest bristlecone pine tree in the world. Its youth belies its significance, for it is also a signpost on the environmental highway—a beacon of change.

Trees growing in and around the Patriarch Grove are about half the age of those in the Schulman Grove, which lies about a thousand feet (305 m) lower in elevation. It seems that the last ice age, which ended here about twelve thousand years ago, forced the bristlecone pines down to a tolerable climate at a lower elevation. As Earth slowly warmed, trees began to migrate back up from their "retreated" lower elevations. Eventually this upward migration reached its apex in and around the Patriarch Grove. Thus, the trees at lower elevations have been growing for a longer period than these upper-elevation "newcomers," with bristlecone pines in and around the visitor center having reached astonishingly old ages.

There is another interesting side to this story of bristlecone migration. The upper limit of a tree line is determined by temperature rather than precipitation. The increase in global temperatures worldwide has forced young bristlecones to germinate and migrate at accelerated rates up the mountain face and across the Patriarch Grove. This has created a virtual nursery of juvenile trees haphazardly scattered across these grounds. It seems as though the higher altitudes are now providing temperatures that are somewhat more welcoming, particularly for young bristlecones. Just as Americans in cold winter country migrate southward to Florida in search of warmer temperatures, so these trees "migrate" upward as the climate warms. Insects such as the bark beetle, which have also moved to significantly higher elevations, provide additional evidence of this persistent warming trend in the White Mountains.

Climatologically severe sites like the Patriarch Grove are difficult places for seeds to germinate and become established. When bristlecone seeds fall, they typically helicopter to the ground, slowly rotating in the still air or beating against rocks and tree trunks in a stiff breeze. Depending upon the prevailing winds, it is not unusual for bristlecone seeds to travel for several miles. Like many varieties of pine trees, grounded seeds become easy prey for foraging birds and small mammals. In addition, they are vulnerable to desiccation in this harsh and arid ecosystem.

However, not all seeds are dependent upon chance for their germination. Birds like Clark's nutcracker (*Nucifraga columbiana*), a gray, black, and white relative of the jay that is common wherever bristlecones grow, often remove bristlecone seeds from their cones. In order to gather and transport those seeds, nutcrackers have a sublingual pouch (an expanded portion of the alimentary tract, primarily in birds, used for storing food) that can hold up to

The Clark's nutcracker is dependent on the seeds of bristlecone pines, just as the trees are dependent on the birds for seed dispersal.

150 seeds. They eat some of those seeds, but they also store others under one or two inches of soil. During the fall months they may bury as many as 98,000 seeds in numerous hidden caches. Most remarkable, however, is the fact that these birds have incredible long-term spatial memory and can locate about 90 percent of cached seeds up to nine months after burying them.

The buried seeds, if not retrieved, can germinate and become seedlings, although overall survival rates of seeds dispersed by wind compared to those dispersed by nutcrackers are unknown. You and I might think it logical that seeds buried at a depth invisible to rodents and protected from drying should survive at a higher rate than those spread willy-nilly over the landscape by random summer gusts. Unfortunately, botanists have no conclusive evidence to support that supposition. For now, I am content to consider this "arrangement" as an excellent example of biological mutualism, a naturally occurring relationship in nature in which each of two organisms benefits. In short, seeds get planted, and birds get food.

The trail encircling the Patriarch Tree is but a quarter-mile (0.4 km) long, and I quickly returned to the parking area and a most welcome bottle of water. Leaning against the car, I looked off to my right and followed the curves of the Cottonwood Basin Overlook Trail as it arcs its way out of the parking area and across a timeless void. The trail winds in and around various boulders as it ascends to a rocky crest encircled by a copse of young bristle-cones. Draining my refreshment, I set off on this half-mile (0.8 km) loop trail, pacing myself for the final ascent.

After crossing a dehydrated landscape, I began a slow climb around massive boulders, over rocky ledges, and past arboreal youngsters just getting their start in this meager ecosystem. The trees here are small now, but they will be here for two to three thousand years or more, long after my footprints disappear from this dusty terrain.

Thirty minutes later I climbed up and across one last boulder, ascended a few more feet in elevation, and arrived at the trail's summit. Like an antiquated steam engine, I was huffing at this oxygen-depleted elevation, at roughly 11,500 feet (3,535 m), but the views were well worth the exhaustion. I could see for 360 degrees in every direction. Like a child on a carnival ride, I turned myself clockwise, methodically rotating in slow circles to take in the splendid outlook.

Sweeping downhill on all sides were long palisades of gnarly bristlecones. I saw rocky outcroppings dotting the topography, and in the faraway distance, regal mountains tinged with green and black. Small marshmallow clouds trekked across the sky in fast-changing patterns. Immediately around were towering peaks, licked by snow, rising into the sapphire sky. And everywhere, in distances both near and far, was a palette of sun-rich colors painting the landscape with brilliant and energetic hues.

My hesitation at the top of the trail was long. The panorama, an outlook awash in brilliant pigments, enraptured me. It was though I was in the middle of an enormous circular IMAX screen, visually bombarded from all sides. This was the peak of visual splendor, a singular perspective across a broad expanse that held beauty and silence.

I slid my way down the backside of the trail and through a broad expanse of enormous boulders and creviced rocks. Below the pinnacle and midway across the descending terrain, I paused before a most impressive bristlecone. Time and weather had given it a crosslike shape, with a twisted trunk, twisted roots, twisted branches. Even in death it stood resplendent, with clear California sunlight glancing off every cranny.

Crossing over the descending terrain, I eventually arrived back at the Patriarch Tree. Keenly alert, I focused once more on it. Not nearly as old as some, but clearly a scion of a distinguished family, it captures the eye and embraces the soul. It is at once beautiful; and to my mind a totem for long and prosperous lives.

The scorching sun, well past its zenith, etched deepening shadows across bald and barren elevations. I reclaimed my car, and on my slow and bumpy journey back down the mountain, I considered the "meeting" between one *Homo sapiens* and a singular *Pinus longaeva*. Long years before, this tree had rooted, inched its way towards sunlight, and sustained itself in an environment that is at once harsh, and yet complimentary. It rose from the bosom of these mountains unaffected by human logic, plan, or design. I was but a brief intruder into its sanctum.

The tree would retain its station; I would travel on.

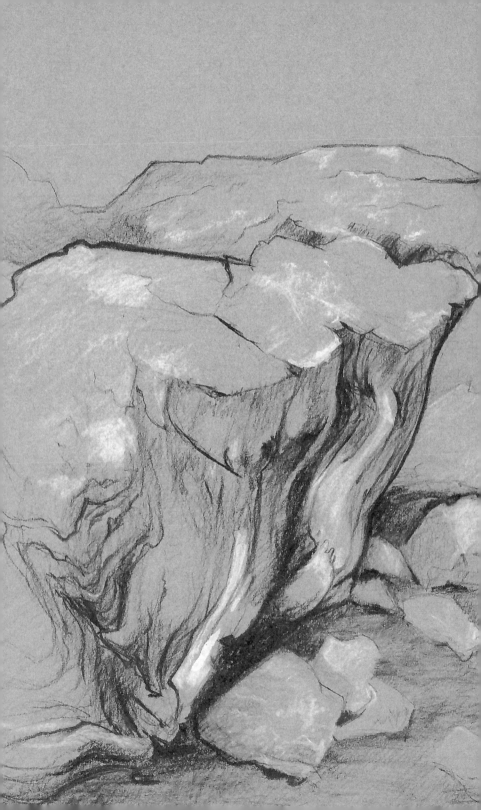

CHAPTER 3

Against a Crooked Sky

Common name: Great Basin bristlecone pine

Scientific binomial: *Pinus longaeva*

Age: 4,844 years

Location: Wheeler Peak, Great Basin National Park, eastern Nevada

2880 BCE, La Plata Basin, Southeastern Uruguay

Ka'kupe and Aratiri were the best of friends. They grew up together, lived in the same homes for more than forty years, and married sisters. Their extended families had celebrated festivals together for decades. Their village was in a wetland area, one that provided an abundant and reliable supply of water.

Scattered nearby were several Ombú (*Phytolacca dioica*) trees, massive evergreens native to Uruguay and Argentina. According to Guaraní legend, the creator, Tupá, gave the Ombú tree a soft and spongy trunk and a large canopy to shelter both animals and humans. Tupá also provided the tree with the gift of immortality. As a result, Ombú trees are known to live for several hundred years.

Ka'kupe and Aratiri worked in the expanding fields surrounding the village. But now a fierce storm was on the horizon, and they needed to finish harvesting the maize crop quickly.

Otherwise the violent winds would flatten the entire field, leaving nothing to harvest.

The first eddies of the approaching storm caused the tops of the maize stalks to waver and bend. It was a sure sign that the weather would soon be on them. Working together, they rapidly pulled ears of maize with practiced hands, tossing them into open baskets. They took them to their granary, where Ka'kupe's oldest daughter scooped handfuls of cobs from each of the baskets and rapidly sorted them into several other baskets inside the enclosure.

The wind picked up, and the two old men dashed through the parallel rows of maize, grabbing cobs, filling baskets. It was a race against the weather, and it seemed as though the wind had the upper hand. Then the hail fell. At first they were tiny balls of ice, but as the storm began its march across this fertile valley, the hailstones grew larger and fell with greater force. Ka'kupe and Aratiri worked at a feverish rate—hobbling, loping, and scrambling between the final few rows of corn. They exchanged no words. Their task was clear, and they had no time to waste.

As fortune would have it, a small group of villagers appeared at the edge of the field. They quickly saw the predicament of the two old men and dispersed without speaking through the field. The wind whipped their hats, and the hailstones pelted them unmercifully. But they too, knew the implications of a lost crop. Each filled baskets to overflowing. Each helped unload the crop just as a brilliant bolt of lightning lit up the sky and stuck the ground at the edge of the field.

2880 BCE, Eastern Nevada

Some 6,305 miles (10,147 km) northwest of Uruguay and its complex farming society the air was crisp and dry. The sun hung over the thirsty landscape like a punishing god bent on revenge against all living things. Creatures both large and small took refuge under boulders, in the crevices of dry river beds, and beneath the arcing branches of wind-swept bushes. Poking up above the desert floor, a massive glacial mountain, which is now part of the South Snake Range, pierced the clouds and crowded the horizon. Its peak, named today after nineteenth-century explorer George Wheeler, ascended to a height of 13,065 feet (3,982 m), the second tallest in Nevada. Composed of numerous ecological zones, it was home then as now to a wide variety of wildlife including mule deer, marmots, coyotes, and jackrabbits. Vegetation comprised multiple species of sagebrush, stands of sharp-needled piñon pines, short-needled junipers, scrappy mountain mahoganies, groves of mixed conifers, red-barked ponderosa pines, aspens, and contorted pines.

An errant seed, perhaps conveyed by prevailing winds, dropped by a parent tree, or secreted in the stomach of a migratory bird, landed on this mountainous landscape. A fortuitous mix of moisture, soil, and abundant sunlight might have been sufficient for the seed to sprout and survive in this severe ecosystem. Decade by patient decade, it pushed its way into the thin atmosphere, and century by persistent century it outlived its contemporaries with resilience and strength.

This large physiographic area was then a mosaic of semiarid basins, scattered mountains, and salt flats. With moderate temperatures, it produced perennial streams and sweeping ponderosa pine forests, particularly at higher elevations. Low shrubs and spreading tufts of grass dominated the landscape. Groups collectively known as the Great Basin Desert Archaic people would colonize it in time. They hunted animals such as mule deer and antelope and collected wild plants such as onions, wild rye, and piñon pine nuts. They also used grinding stones to process plant seeds into flour and meal. Additionally, they made baskets, mats, hats, and sandals from plant fibers and used animal hides to make their clothes and moccasins. Marine shell beads are also associated with this cultural period, indicating trade and communication with coastal peoples farther west.

Present Day

A forty-minute drive from where I live is Gifford Pinchot State Park, one of the jewels in the Pennsylvania state park system (124 state parks comprising more than 300,000 acres). Highlighted by a 340-acre lake and surrounded by bucolic camping spaces, extensive recreational facilities, loads of picnicking spots, and a tranquility far removed from the bustle of urban life, it is one of our favorite escapes. From spring through autumn, we journey to the lake, walk well-trod trails along the perimeter, and picnic under lofty branches in one of the park's numerous groves.

On a still and silent spring afternoon, I found myself on the Lakeside Trail, looking in all directions for the tracks of small mammals or the hurried scuttle of ducks. I caught sight of a broken tree that had fallen across the trail sometime during the winter months and had been moved by park rangers to clear the path. They had also chainsawed the base of the tree, leaving a prominent stump along the periphery of the trail. I knelt down and began to count rings. I got to 114 rings before my back informed me that this was a province of younger folks and that senior would-be dendrochronologists should pursue ring counting from the comfort of a well-padded camp chair.

While the field of dendrochronology may be young, scientists often celebrate it as a "hands-on" discipline, one that invites the general public to interact with trees in much the same way as professional dendrochronologists. In truth, it is a tangible field: both you and I can feel the woody interior of a tree as opposed to our inability to touch hydrogen atoms, the fiery magma of volcanoes, or the rings of Saturn. Several dendrochronologists are fond of pointing out that most people are comfortable with the concept behind dendrochronology, having looked at the top of a tree stump as kids (or even as adults) and counting the rings. But few people know what other types of information can be extracted out of those same tree rings. Part of the discipline involves explaining this complex field science to a broad audience, building on discoveries and stories.

As you know, rings tell the story of a tree's life. Those rings convey both history and ecology as an engaging assembly of environmental truths and compelling narratives. A forest of trees is a library of rich tales, a compendium of wisdom. Dendrochronology, as shared earlier, is a door to the past, an entrée into things unknown, and a collection of eye-opening tales. The following is one of dendrochronology's most famous—or rather, infamous—stories. Unfortunately, this one doesn't have a happy ending.

Great Basin National Park lies just outside of the remote eastern Nevada town of Baker. In this park, visitors travel through another world, dimension, and, most certainly another time. Great Basin is a showcase for Nevada's geographical diversity. While it may be one of the least visited in the national park system, it is certainly one of the most expansive. Here visitors will discover a high desert that crisply accents some of the state's tallest peaks. At the top of Wheeler Peak, a vista of gray-cast mountains, sage-covered foothills, and the solitude of wilderness greet them. Great Basin has the state's only remaining glacier, an assembly of pulsating mountain streams, crystal blue alpine lakes, groves of ancient bristlecone pines, and the state's largest cave system. It is an ecological paradise that attracts a wide range of worldwide visitors, including hikers, fishers, campers, and stargazers. Years ago, it also attracted an inexperienced scientist who may have made the biggest mistake ever committed in dendrochronological history.

It was the summer of 1964, and a young geographer, Donald Currey, was investigating ice age glaciology, exploring the geological features in eastern Nevada's Snake Range, where he sought out the magnificent bristlecone pines. He directed his attention specifically on the Wheeler Peak scenic area, a tract of land that seemingly harbored some of the oldest trees in the country, if not the world. The area was windy and littered with massive boulders and reaches of limestone soil, and the air was thin and oxygen-poor. But the anticipation of a career-enhancing discovery drove the young scientist on his quest.

Armed with his Swedish increment borer, Currey sampled numerous bristlecones along the mountain's slopes. Each sampling required him to insert his borer into the trunk of a tree, screw it slowly and methodically into the wood near the base of the tree, usually the thickest part, and then reverse the twisting process to remove a pencil-thin segment of the tree up to twenty-eight inches (71 cm) long. A scientist would place that specimen under a microscope and methodically count the rings, both fat and slim, one by one to determine the overall age of the tree, or at least provide a very close estimate.

It was a labor-intensive job. The borer had to be hand-twisted into the trunk of a four-thousand-year-old tree, which required enormous strength and patience. And then, just as methodically, the borer was reverse twisted to remove the ring sample from the heart of the tree. Currey devoted his days to obtaining several different core samples, his evenings to intensive examinations of those samples to determine their overall age, variations in the width of the rings, and patterns of good and bad growing seasons. He suspected these particular trees were repositories of vast amounts of climatic information, a storehouse of weather data that would provide clues to an ever-changing ecosystem.

After several days on the mountain, Currey located a tree at a point roughly 10,750 feet (3,277 m) in elevation. Forest historian Eric Rutkow writes that Currey's 114th specimen was the most spectacular that he had encountered. He measured it as having a

252-inch (6.4 m) circumference eighteen inches (46 cm) above the ground. Currey also noted that the tree's bark, which was necessary for its survival, was only present along a single nineteen-inch (48 cm)-wide, north-facing strip. The winds and sand had worn away everything else. But the tree was alive and still producing compact bunches of needles on a three-inch-wide shoot. The tree, known to local mountaineers as Prometheus, seemed perfect for boring.

It was the morning of August 6, 1964. Now, some of the principal players have passed away, memories of select events have faded over time, and a few details may have shifted here and there in the story's retellings, but what we do know is that shortly after Currey began his sampling his borer broke. He obtained a substitute borer and tried again to twist into the dense wood. Again, that borer broke. Currey quickly realized that without his borers, there was no way he could accurately determine the age of the tree. Unless he cut it down.

The young scientist reached out and requested permission from the local district Forest Service ranger to fell the tree. After consulting with his supervisor, the ranger granted Currey the permission he needed to topple the tree. A work crew, large saws in hand, cut into the trunk, and several hours later the tree fell to the ground, leaving a large, broad stump with its characteristic rings clearly visible as its remaining signature. Later that day, Currey placed several cross-sections of the tree under his microscope and began to count. After several hours, the count revealed that Prometheus contained 4,847 growth rings. Because of the harsh conditions in which these trees grow, it is likely a growth ring did not form every year. As a result, scientists estimated Prometheus to be approximately 4,900 years old, the oldest known tree at the time. Rutkow elaborates that Currey had unintentionally felled the most ancient tree ever discovered, an organism that

A cut stump reveals annual rings. Wide or narrow,
they record the tree's entire life.

was old when Columbus reached Hispaniola, passing through
middle age when Caesar ruled Rome, and beginning its life when
the Sumerians created the first written language.

When Currey published the results of his discovery in
the professional journal *Ecology*, he ventured that WPN-114, the
scientific name of the tree, was the oldest tree on record. He
speculated that additional discoveries across the mountain would
most likely reveal much older trees in the future. However, that
brief, three-page article sparked controversy, with critics charging
that Currey had disrupted a delicate ecosystem. It also generated
discussions and arguments about our ecological responsibilities,
with diverse opinions still found in the literature more than a
half-century later.

You and I might argue that no tree under the protection of the
US Forest Service should be felled. How disingenuous, we might
say, for the guardians of forests to offer both permission and

opportunity to eliminate the very organisms they protect. That the Forest Service had acted recklessly and without regard for its ultimate mission flies in the face of both logic and scientific principle. Those arguments strongly suggest that the apparently indiscriminate cutting of the oldest known tree was in violation of natural events and dendrochronological protocols.

We might argue that this was just one tree in an ocean of trees spread across the North American continent. We might opine that it was located in a distant and almost inaccessible location— one seldom visited. Surrounded by a sea of ancient boulders and the brain-numbing altitude of Wheeler Peak it was of little consequence, little notice. How could one tree make a difference? Why should we care about a tree located in the middle of nowhere in a location we'll never visit or remember? There are millions of other trees, in thousands of other forests, in scores of easily reached locations for me to see.

Still others, overflowing with anger and rage, demean Currey and those who supported his actions as anti-environmentalists. The loss of a single tree is just the tip of the proverbial iceberg, an ecological expanse under siege, bit by bit, and acre by acre. Where do we stop? How do we curb the deforestation of the continent if we can't protect a single tree? Or perhaps the bigger question revolves around our role as caretakers of the earth and the impact that the felling of a single tree that is as old as written history says about our earthly priorities, with the sad fact that the often-callous inquiry of humans frequently results in the felling of living trees in order to obtain "necessary" scientific data at the expense of their longevity.

While this story does not end happily, it is also a signpost on the environmental highway. It is a chapter in a much larger narrative about what is worth preserving and what is worth studying. It is also a story about the interactions of humans upon and within their world. Perhaps the question becomes, "What is our ongoing relationship with trees, and how will that relationship, in the future, impact the survival and/or existence of both forests and trees?"

According to ancient Greek mythology, Prometheus was an immortal who brought fire, which is symbolic of knowledge, to humans, and the gods punished him for eternity for the theft. Prometheus the tree also imparted knowledge to humans, but at a price. Sadly, it is only recently that we have righted that wrong. The remaining bristlecone pines on Wheeler Peak are now protected for as long as there is a United States. As a sidenote, it may be worth noting that Currey, in atonement for his arboreal sin, championed national park status for Great Basin.

Walk along the Wheeler Peak Summit Trail, a 4.3-mile (6.9 km), 3,000 vertical foot (914 m) Class 1 hike, and a 360-degree panorama of rugged extremes will greet you: a large glacial cirque, enormous moraines, and an active rock glacier along with the silence of time. So, too, will you be able to gaze across a simmering talus field descending downward and across the face of this expanse. Here, you will discover random stands of bristlecones clinging to life under turquoise skies. In so many ways, this is a spiritual community, a council of magnificent beings that have weathered elements and survived the centuries with determination. As with any population, its strength is in its resilience and its stand for what is right. Sometimes, though, outsiders intervene.

It is in this territory that the sad and weathered stump of Prometheus stands inside a verdant grouping of well-aged trees. The stump barely rises above the substrate, surrounded by a slew of gray boulders, occasional, green-needled neighbors, and scattered scraps of its once and complete existence. Pale and sun-baked, it is a remnant of time and a marker of a once-robust being.

After your mountain visit, take your own personal journey back through history by counting the rings of Prometheus. You can do so at the Great Basin National Park visitor center. There, you will encounter a display entitled "A Life Story." With a magnifying glass positioned over a two-inch thick sawed-off remnant, interpretive signage tells this story in brief:

This tree, named Prometheus, was more than 4,900 years old when it was cut down for research purposes in 1964.

It began life around the same time that the pyramids of Giza were built. As it grew, the Roman Empire rose and fell, Mayan cities boomed and collapsed, and the Ming Dynasty came and went. This section has about 2,920 rings, representing about 2,920 years of the tree's life. Each inch of the slab represents about 54 years.

Also included as part of the display is an absorbing chronology of events that took place during the lifetime of this tree. It is an almanac of a life cut short as well as a commemoration of a life lived long. For some, it speaks to a traumatic intersection of science and history. For others, it is a reminder of the hubris of humans whose lessons, too often, come late and often at the expense of the natural world and its respectable denizens. It is a Greek tragedy for modern times.

Part II

Into the
Forest

Forests are a permanent part of the world as much as they are a permanent part of our lives. We walk between their splendid trunks, gaze up into their canopies, and admire their spread across multiple landscapes. We unfold our picnic blankets beneath their branches, gaze with rapt admiration at their changing hues in autumn, and honor them with superlatives and titles befitting royal lineage. They are exemplars of social networks, congregations of individuals that work in concert for a common good and a common survival.

In the chapters that follow you will meet some remarkable forests that have not only stood tall against the perils of time but have also distinguished themselves as idyllic figures of grace and resolution. As biological bastions, they have grown old together. They have endured elements that, quite often, take down entire populations of timbers, and, they have bested the challenges of nature.

Here you will encounter the largest and oldest tree in existence—a single tree disguised as a forest—that has faced all manner of strife and lived quite well. You will meet the tallest trees in the world, which now inhabit a very narrow slice of northern California geography, trees that suck great quantities of their nourishment from passing clouds. You will experience a languorous drift down an ebony river in North Carolina as it weaves its way through shrouded trees and their knobby knees. And you will walk between the massive and imposing trunks of sequoias whose lives are anything but calm and tranquil. They, too, have survived long demanding years.

These journeys into glorious enclaves of longevity offer myriad opportunities to experience both the beauty and wisdom of forests. These ventures will open your eyes and your mind to some of the world's most amazing stories. You will touch history, encounter worlds of wonder, and remember communities of beings with roots that extend deep into the past.

CHAPTER 4

Touching Clouds

Common name: Coast redwood

Scientific binomial: *Sequoia sempervirens*

Age: 2,000+ years

Location: Coastal California from the Oregon border to south of Monterey Bay

479 BCE, Egypt, 10 Miles (16 km) South of Cairo

Khafra and Thutmose, two high-ranking priests, had been accorded a great honor, selected to mummify the recently deceased pharaoh along with his cherished cat. As soon as the pharaoh's body arrived at the temple, the two lifted it onto a special table inclined to allow the body fluids to drain away. After several hours, the purification process could begin. First Thutmose washed the deceased with sacred water. Then Khafra fumigated the body with terebinth resin drawn from *Pistacia terebinthus*, a deciduous conifer 23 feet (7 m) tall native to North Africa. The resin of the tree, often referred to as turpentine, has antifungal and antimicrobial characteristics that make it ideal for long-term mummification. Afterward, the priests cleaned the remains with oils, spices, and essences. Finally, using ritual instruments, they removed all the body hair.

Next Thutmose opened the skull. Using a specially shaped spoon along with other instruments and some caustic acids, he carefully extracted chunks of the brain. Once he had emptied the cranial box, Thutmose rinsed it with palm oil and stuffed it with strips of linen and liquefied resin. Then Khafra took a long-bladed knife and made a deep incision on the left flank of the body. With practiced hands, he removed all the viscera. Thutmose joined him and carefully rinsed the inside of the body with palm wine. Afterward the two priests filled the empty body cavities with a combination of myrrh, cinnamon, and other perfumes. Then they carefully sewed up the body with fine thread. In silence, they washed the viscera in palm wine. They cleaned each of the organs, encased them in crushed herbs, and placed them in ceremonial canopic jars.

Next the two priests pulled a large ceramic jar of natron over to the embalming table. A naturally occurring mineral often found on the bottom of dry lake beds, natron was critical in Egyptian mummification ceremonies because it is an effective desiccant. They carefully spread the mineral over every body part to dry the flesh and eliminate potential putrefaction. They then placed the body on a ceremonial table, where it would rest for forty days.

Afterward, the two priests oiled the corpse with special fragrances and lubricants. They augmented facial features, fingers, and toes with a rich combination of ceremonial paints and added a special wig. Next they spread a henna-based antiseptic over the skin to give it a more lifelike appearance. This ointment further prevented any molds or fungi that might destroy the flesh.

Then they began the wrapping. First they laid various jewelry items and amulets given to them by the pharaoh's family across the skin. They placed the pharaoh's arms alongside his body. Then the two priests wrapped the entire body from head to toe in long strips of flax. The final step was the ceremony of the Opening of the Mouth. This procedure, which involved no fewer than seventy-five different stages, would bring the deceased back to life, or so the Egyptians believed. Finally they placed a ceremonial mask carved by a local carpenter over the face of the deceased.

The mummy would last for centuries.

479 BCE, Northern California

At the same time as that mummification process was taking place, an unnoticed event happened 7,296 miles (11,741 km) to the northwest. A tiny seed, no larger than that of a tomato, found its way into the rich soil in a land inhabited by nomadic tribes of hunters. There it would sprout and grow into a tremendous tree, a tree that throngs of adventurers would admire for both its magnificence and its ancient roots some 2,500 years later.

A vast territory of steep canyons, meandering streams, alluvial terraces, and fern-lined valleys hugged the Pacific coastline. This impressive environment featured elevation ranges from sea level to 3,200 feet (975 m). Annual rainfall between sixty and one hundred inches (1.5–2.54 m) bathed the northern part of the range. The irregular expanse of littoral terrain that twisted its way southward had much less rainfall but equal diverse flora and fauna. This land of magnificent redwood forests—towering, impressive, and majestic trees—soared to the clouds, emblematic of nature's majesty.

For thousands of years, Indigenous peoples from a wide variety of tribes including the Yurok, Karuk, Tolowa, Wiyot, Chilula, Whilkut, and Hupa inhabited this vibrant environment. They fished the salmon-rich rivers that cascaded down from snow-crusted mountains and hunted the deer and elk that resided in the darkened corners of the forest. Periodic harvesting of nuts, berries, and seeds and other natural foods supplemented their diet. Crops such as squash and beans were also an integral part of their plentiful diet. The native peoples of the region were capable hunters, fishers, gatherers, and farmers, helping them evade the cycles of feast and famine that marked less generous ecosystems.

Villages dotted the landscape, primarily beside the numerous streams and rivers, and occupied several locations along the turbulent coast. Even though politics and geography separated the enclaves, trade routes, social interactions, and economic factors linked them. Spiritual beliefs often centered on the role of nature and the necessary of maintaining the wealth of resources at their disposal. They were a people in delicate balance with the land.

Present Day

On my first visit to explore the trees of Redwood State and National Parks, I stood in awe. I was amazed by the titans that soared skyward in splendid groves. Every step through this forested wonderland of deep valleys and winding trails revealed their splendor.

My most recent venture was equally awe-inspiring. On this trip, my wife and I visited Founders' Grove in Humboldt Redwoods State Park. The veils of ferns and vaulting trees felt like a scene out of a European fairytale. Various shades of green were scattered across the forest floor under vibrant and resilient ancient trees. I approached one tree and assumed the classic "tree hugger" pose, trying to wrap my arms around its base. I quickly calculated that with a personal "wingspan" of about six feet (1.8 m) it would take at least five arm spreads to encircle the circumference. The number of downed trees was equally interesting, as though a giant hand swatted select trees and cast them asunder. It was a most interesting punctuation mark on their vitality; yes, they live for thousands of years, but eventually they will fall. Among this detritus, however, were persistent signs of new generations of life: ferns growing out of withered and uprooted roots, with moss, fungi, and lichens gracing their trunks.

A lone banana slug tugged its way over the forest floor on a mission to seek sustenance or a potential mate. Surrounded by environmental guards that loomed tall against the sky, it cared little about my intrusion. The slug's genetic code dictated its mission. I watched as the slug methodically continued its journey under a broken redwood twig, up and over a clump of forest duff, and past a stand of ferns.

Later I discovered a tree that had succumbed to the ravages of fire, age, weather, climate, and violent cycles of lightning. Lying prone on the damp earth, it revealed a charred exterior in addition to blankets of moss growing along its trunk. Sprouts popped up along its upper flange, signals that perhaps there was still some life in this archaic giant. The sun disappeared for the day leaving only late shadows and grays in the sky overhead. My wife and I walked over a small wooden bridge, across a creek, and into an expanse of ascending fernery that would not have been out of place in the Jurassic period. I half-expected a band of sauropods to lumber through the forest and past my station.

Redwoods are a "bucket list" experience. The ability of redwoods to arouse awe is one of their signature features and leaves a memory that never departs the soul. Most people, including me, walk through a redwood forest and discover an inability to find sufficient adjectives for them. These visual experiences lie beyond the realm of language.

A sign near the Big Tree Wayside in the Prairie Creek Redwoods State Park bears a Yurok legend:

How the redwood came to be

Before people arrived on earth, there was a race of divine Spirit Beings (Woge) who lived here and who, by their actions, instituted the rules and behavior by which people and all other beings must live. When humans arrived, some Woge transformed themselves into certain animals, plants, and features on the landscape. The creators—Pulekukwerek and Wohpekumeu—talked together and did not know how people would cross the river. They had no wood. Then suddenly one of the Woge, who grew up quickly there, said, "That is what I came for. I can be used for homes. I can be used for boats. They will make boats of me and cross the river. I am called Keehl (redwood)." Pulekukwerek said, "It is good that you grew so quickly. Now people will live properly."

As we walked along the winding trail behind the sign, I was reminded that this forest, indeed all redwood forests, have a long history. Redwoods once covered most of what we now know as the Northern Hemisphere. The first redwood fossils are indeed remnants of the Jurassic period, a time when gigantic reptiles reigned.

Humans arrived millions of years later, coastal people who used redwood lumber to build houses, create tools, and to construct canoes. Later, prospectors and entrepreneurs, propelled by the California Gold Rush and the insatiable need for lumber to build towering San Francisco mansions, wide-valley bridges, vast commercial enterprises, and rapidly expanding communities arrived. The lure of earthen riches brought hundreds of thousands of Euro-Americans to this territory. When they came, there were approximately two million acres (809,400 ha) of redwoods. A robust advertising campaign proclaimed redwoods as the "wonder wood," and loggers swept in to seize the bounty. Trees fell in increasing numbers over the ensuing decades, transformed into churches, train cars, furniture, household goods, musical instruments, football stadiums, piers, trestles, pipelines, guardrails, and even septic tanks. In the late nineteenth and early twentieth centuries, if it could be built with wood, redwood typically figured. Loggers stripped once-vibrant forests. Stands of giant trees that had lived for centuries vanished, transformed into goods and bric-a-brac of every dimension and purpose.

Today, only 5 percent of the original forests remains.

The growth of a redwood tree is nothing short of miraculous. Frequently characterized as one of the fastest growing trees on the planet, young redwoods have established botanical speed records in terms of both height and girth. However, they concentrate much of their maturation process on moving upward, escaping shadows that play along the forest floor and ascending past slower-growing trees and shrubs that might hinder or complicate their growth. Redwoods, which can live to be two thousand years old and more, achieve most of their vertical ascent within their first hundred years. During that time, a coast redwood may grow three to ten feet (0.9–3 m) per year and one inch (2.5 cm) in trunk diameter annually. This is when a tree experiences its most rapid period of development. Thus, by the time a tree is between one hundred and two hundred years old its tip may be near the outer edge of the canopy, about 200 to 350 feet (61–107 m) above the forest floor.

Once a redwood tree reaches the canopy, it lives under conditions of increased sunlight, more violent winds, and lower humidity levels. Its growth pattern changes. Vertical growth slows, and the tree now invests its energy in expanding its girth. Several research studies have indicated that, on average, a two-hundred-year-old tree will have a trunk three to five feet (0.9–1.5 m) in diameter. That measurement will increase to five to seven feet (1.5–2.1 m) by the time the tree is four hundred years old, and it is not unusual for a seven-hundred-year-old redwood to have a trunk diameter of up to fifteen feet (4.6 m).

On a journey into the depths of Lady Bird Johnson Grove just beyond the small town of Orick, I paused before a giant. Here stood a singular tree that severely stretched the limits of my cervical vertebrae. My eyes rolled up the towering height of this tree. They never reached the top, lost in a dense canopy of surrounding trees that inched their way toward the clouds. I could only guess at its height.

In August 2006, naturalists Chris Atkins and Michael Taylor discovered a singular coast redwood in a remote section of Redwood National Park. Using laser equipment, they measured the tree at 379.7 feet (116 m) in height. They named it Hyperion, meaning "he who walks on high." Later that same year, Steve Sillett of Humboldt State University (now Cal Poly Humboldt) climbed to the top of the tree and dropped a tape measure to the ground to confirm its height. Sillett believes this tree is relatively young, around six hundred years of age, and that it is still growing.

Hyperion is at least 74 feet (22.5 m) taller than the Statue of Liberty, 107 feet (32.6 m) taller than the Brooklyn Bridge, and 320 feet (97.5 m) taller than the presidential faces on Mount Rushmore. Redwood trees are nature's grandest construction, in both height and appreciation.

Like some of its tall contemporaries, Hyperion is unusual in that it grows on a mountain slope rather than in an alluvial valley where water would be more abundant. As such, it is in a place where dendrochronologists and foresters might not be looking for tall trees. It is quite possible that there might be even taller redwoods than Hyperion, but they haven't been located yet simply because they might be where they are not expected.

Although the precise location of this giant is unpublished and uncirculated, an ever-increasing number of determined visitors reach it nevertheless. In the process, those interlopers have damaged the habitat leading up to Hyperion, created their own trails, and left trash and human waste along the way. In July 2022, California's Redwood National Park urged visitors to stay away from Hyperion and the area around it. Those who attempt to visit the tree risk a $5,000 fine and up to six months in jail. "As a visitor, you must decide if you will be a part of the preservation of this unique landscape—or will you be part of the destruction?" the Park wrote in an accompanying, and most emphatic, statement.

This tree is fortunate. A few hundred feet from the tree's location are signs of an approaching clearcut, in which loggers remove all the trees in an area. Approximately two weeks before loggers would have cut down Hyperion, President Jimmy Carter added the valley in which it is located to Redwood National Park.

The height of this giant is all the more remarkable when you consider that five of the tallest trees in the world are located within a relatively narrow strip of ecology. Following Hyperion in height are the redwood specimens: Helios (Redwood National Park) at 375.9 feet (114.5 m), Icarus (Redwood National Park) at 371.2 feet (113 m), Stratosphere Giant (Humboldt Redwoods State Park) at 370.9 feet (113 m), and National Geographic (Redwood National Park) at 369.8 feet (112.7 m). Equally amazing is the fact that at least 180 known redwoods ascend to heights greater than 350 feet (106.6 m). Scientists remeasure most of the tallest trees at intervals of no more than three years and recalculate the very tallest annually, so that these reported heights and rankings will likely change over the years.

Most visitors to Redwood National and State Parks cant their heads upward at a forty-five-degree angle, taking long skyward pauses on calendar-perfect forest trails, uttering exclamations full of amazement and admiration. As most will agree, much of the awesomeness of redwoods lies in their stature. Often soaring to unimaginable heights, their crowns scrape powder blue skies and their tips brush through moisture-laden clouds curving in from the Pacific.

Beyond their physical measure, they are also astoundingly old.

One of the questions often asked of rangers throughout the various redwood parks is, "How old do these trees get?" The short answer is that coast redwoods normally live between five hundred and fifteen hundred years, with a few individuals crossing beyond two thousand. These life spans are highly dependent on an array of environmental adaptations that allow redwoods to attain these long lives.

The redwood species has been on this planet for approximately 240 million years. Redwoods have been extant since the age of dinosaurs and once covered a substantial portion of the Earth's surface. They have existed in California for approximately 20 million years, long before humans traveled into their forests. Yet in the past 150 years of this country's history, logging, land development, and other human activities have dramatically reduced the number of these formidable trees.

Although redwoods cannot stand up to the persistence of chain saws, skidders, forwarders, feller bunchers, or delimbers, a unique set of genetic factors offer them protection against some of nature's ravages. One of the signature features of redwoods is their ability to access necessary moisture. Their location along the northern California coast provides abundant rain during the winter months in addition to thick fogs in summer months. Redwoods have the unique ability to snare fog on their leaves. That captured fog condenses into drops and is either absorbed by the needles or falls to the ground as a light rain.

Very tall trees face the challenge of having to transport water from their roots up to their topmost reaches. A gallon (3.79 l) of water weighs about 8.3 pounds (3.7 kg), depending on temperature. A single redwood tree uses more than 150 gallons (568 l) of water per day in the summer, 40 percent of which is from fog. That's 1,245 pounds (565 kg) of water. A tree needs to lift the water necessary for its survival to a height of 350 feet (106.6 m) or more. Redwoods are able to overcome the power of gravity as the result of a morphological adaptation in their needles. Needles near the top of a redwood are awl-like and absorbent, which gives them better water retention. As a result, the topmost needles can trap the rolling ocean fog directly into their leaves.

Abundant organic tannins and terpenoids throughout the trees also play a role in the longevity of redwoods. (We will learn more about tannins in chapter 7.) These naturally occurring chemicals ward off insects, fungal rot, as well as an array of arboreal diseases. The bark, with little flammable pitch, also has tannins, a chemical element which not only makes the tree disease-resistant, but also acts as a naturally occurring fire retardant. A fire in and of itself is not immediately dangerous for a redwood. However, a series of fires over the lifetime of a tree creates a succession of burn scars that eventually deepen and progress through the bark. This allows fungi to enter the heartwood, or center of the tree, and over time they sufficiently weaken it.

As redwoods age, they also contend with a variety of environmental pressures and infirmities. Quite often redwoods succumb to root or stem rot. This severely weakens the tree, leaving it vulnerable to breakage by gravity, wind, flood, or fire. Often these tall trees, weighing in excess of twenty-five tons (22,680 kg), develop a lean—a gravitational tilt that, over time, gets increasingly more acute. Eventually the tree breaks or topples. This typically happens during gargantuan storms when fierce winds stress the crown, and the water-soaked soil is unable to grasp the roots sufficiently to hold a tree in place. If a particular tree lives on a floodplain or adjacent to a stream, erosion from swift flowing waters may undercut the root system and in time topple it.

Then there are the ecological accidents. These include those times when an ancient tree, as the result of several factors, falls, crashing through one or more neighboring trees and injuring them so that they can no longer stand. I recall seeing an enormous giant along Prairie Creek that had succumbed to several infirmities. It must have crashed to the ground in a crescendo of thunder and noise. As it fell, it took down nearly a dozen of its neighbors, leaving an arboreal graveyard of both old and young specimens. As I stood beside this enormous wreckage, I noted that all of the downed trees had since sprouted a variety of vegetation including ferns, small saplings, and an ever-present carpet of moss along their now horizontal lengths. One tree's demise had created a micro-ecosystem that furthered and extended the life of the forest.

She stood on the edge of US 101, watching cars and trucks pass by at speeds of 60 miles per hour (97 km/h) or more. Suddenly, and without warning, she stepped onto the roadway and walked to the center lane. She paused, seemingly unconcerned by the approaching traffic. We were northbound, about to make a left-hand turn onto the scenic Newton B. Drury Parkway. My wife gently applied the brakes and pulled to the side of the busy roadway. We watched as two other individuals equally unconcerned by the line of cars approaching their station in the middle of the highway arrived. Satisfied that their crossing would be safe, they ambled to the other side of the road. Within moments, the other members of this herd of Roosevelt elk joined them in their passage across the bustling highway. Approximately forty-five adults and fawns ambled past our car, occasionally staring at us as they moved from one verdant meadow across the road to the other. After about five minutes, their passage complete, they fanned out across the green grass and began to nibble on it.

The herd of elk reminded me that a redwood forest is a rich and diverse ecosystem, one filled with and sustained by a variety of lifeforms. In addition to elk, which favor prairie and other open lands but seek the redwood forests for cover and shade, the parks are home to salmon, trout, mountain lions, bobcats, coyotes, foxes, black-tailed deer, raptors, owls, gophers, meadow mice, and black bears. An abundance of amphibians and insects also inhabit mature redwood forests. It is an ecosystem of interdependencies, each species reliant on others for survival.

The long-term victory of redwoods and their distinctive ecosystems owes in large measure to the efforts of the Save the Redwoods League. Founded in 1918, the League is a nonprofit organization singularly focused on protecting ancient redwoods. In its tenure, Save the Redwoods League has protected more than 200,000 acres (80,900 ha) of redwood forests and helped create sixty-six redwood parks. The League accomplishes this by purchasing redwood forests and the surrounding land needed to nurture them. The League also restores redwood forests with innovative science and technology that can improve stewardship and accelerate forest regeneration. The League is well known for its embrace of the principles of conservation biology, its ongoing research efforts, and its improvement of a collective understanding and appreciation of redwoods. "We have touched the lives of hundreds of millions of people by connecting them to nature," the League proclaims.

I wanted to gain additional insight into the Save the Redwoods League and its mission, so I caught up with Paul Ringgold, its chief program officer. Ringgold oversees all land conservation transactions, land stewardship and management activities, forest restoration, public funding, policy engagement, park support, and education and interpretive programs. Gregarious and personable, Ringgold has conservationism running through his veins. For him, it is both passion and his life's work. One of my initial questions centered on why the public should care about the League.

Ringgold made the point that the Save the Redwoods League brings extensive experience, background, and history to their work in preserving the redwood forests. He went on to underscore the work it has charted for its next hundred years, ensuring the protection of as much of the remaining redwood forest as possible. "We want to basically double the number of protected reserves within the redwood range," he told me. "And then beyond that, we want to basically protect the rest, at least from conversion to other uses and to heighten forest practices wherever we can."

Ringgold emphasized that the Save the Redwoods League is the only organization that dedicates itself exclusively to redwood forest conservation. Not only is it focused on the permanent protection of redwoods, but it is also concerned about making sure that this protection is based on clear, sound science. He told me that the League recently completed a project to decode the entire genome of redwoods, so that it now has a platform for future understanding of genetic variation and native genetics versus nonnative genetics within the forest stands.

Ringgold emphasized that the League cooperates with other conservation groups. These include partnerships with public agencies as well as other conservation organizations that work within overlapping territories. Ringgold also pointed out that the League has an ongoing study called "The Redwoods in the Climate Change Initiative," in which it has identified sections that will help us understand the long-term impacts of climate change. To do this, teams of scientists climb into the canopies of these trees to measure the biomass associated with redwood foliage, their branches, and the stem. Additionally, increment quarters—borings into the trees with very narrow corers—allow scientists to understand how trees' growth rates have changed over time depending on climate conditions.

A quick observation of the Save the Redwoods League's website and its overwhelming abundance of resources, scientific and general articles, lessons, insights, perspectives, and outreach efforts identifies this organization with both a clearly defined goal and the resources to make it happen. In my conversation with Ringgold, it quickly became apparent that the League was interested not only in improving the overall health and vitality of redwoods throughout their range but also in ensuring that that vitality would become a centerpiece of its efforts well into the future.

To do that, the League recognizes that one of the critical determinants of redwoods' environmental success is a complete comprehension of their age. Garrison Frost, director of communications, put it this way: "Tree rings are not just telling us the age of trees, but also how a tree is growing in response to climate change, how much carbon it is storing, and lots of other valuable information."

That dating process is the surest way of determining a specific tree's age and environmental history. Unfortunately, the largest increment borers can extend only about three feet into a tree, which is not long enough to reach the center of a truly mammoth tree. Redwood experts from Cal Poly Humboldt have figured out a method around this that involves collecting a series of cores up the height of tree every thirty to sixty feet (~6–18 m) or so, comparing rings and radii and using cross-dating to ensure that there are no "missing" rings.

As a result of those dendrochronological investigations, scientists have identified singular redwoods with extended lifetimes. These individual trees, though now dead, give us insight into their protracted life spans. Scientists meticulously measured the rings of one redwood tree that fell in 1994 or thereabouts, most likely because of a storm. Counting revealed 2,026 sequential rings, and scientists noted that the total may have been an underestimate of sample age owing to the possibility of missing rings, a number of very small rings (only two to three cells wide), and some degree of decay. In 2013, scientists scanned and cross-dated a log in Humboldt Redwoods State Park. It had achieved a life span of approximately 2,266 years, extending from 385 BCE to 1881 CE. Another downed tree, cross-dated in 1996, had a reported ring-counted age of 2,200 years. A redwood cross-section on display at the visitor center in Henry Cowell State Park in Santa Cruz has 1,935 rings.

In the late 1980s an adventurous group of college students did something never done before. Taking enormous risks, they used rudimentary climbing equipment to clamber up into the canopies of several towering redwoods. There they discovered a previously unexplored realm, a lost world that was dangerous, mysterious, and expansive. As these daring explorers ventured into the heights, they observed an Eden of mosses, lichens, spotted salamanders, hanging gardens of ferns, thickets of huckleberry bushes, and critters typically consigned to much lower ecosystems. Here were massive trunk systems that formed flying buttresses. The students discovered crotches and limbs, collection traps of falling needles and other debris. This material formed humus mats up to 265 feet (81 m) above the ground. Hundreds of plants including mosses, lichen, huckleberries, and even other full-sized trees have been subsequently found living in the canopies of redwoods. These elevated mats are habitats for many animals typically found on the forest floor. The adventurers observed previously unseen animals such as eagles, owls, salamanders, woodpeckers, woodrats, chipmunks, bumblebees, bats, slugs, and beetles, to name a few, living high above the ground—a bionetwork far higher than previously reported in scientific journals, a natural complex thriving high above the forest floor and far from human eyes.

On one of my early journeys into these groves I gathered information for a children's book, *Tall Tall Tree*, a paean to redwood trees. My task was to create a manuscript revealing the rich ecology of redwoods through rhyme and numeration. So too, was it to be a literary journey into the canopies of these magnificent organisms, an exploration of life forms previously unknown. The

Humus mats and the organisms that live on them are often found high in the branches of redwood trees.

book's subsequent and most positive reception over the ensuing years underscores youngsters' embrace of these most amazing trees.

Whether ascending these tall timbers or standing on the forest, many have discovered that redwoods are repositories of captivating scientific information and dynamic revelations. So, too, do they offer insights about life in general, embedded in their soaring trunks and vibrant canopies. For it is among the redwoods that we can learn important lessons: the value of solitude, a compassion for living organisms, a respect for natural history, an appreciation for biological longevity, a desire for environmental preservation, and ecological humility. In the company of redwoods, we have opportunity to step away from the cacophony of daily living and reconnect with things wondrously normal and contemplatively natural, a reacquaintance with a truer ebb and flow of life. In my own ventures, I discovered that a redwood forest is a pedagogical gift, a classroom brimming with ecological insights and the transformative capture of nature. Standing in a circle of redwood trees beside the canyon that cradles Prairie

Creek or resting beside a towering giant perched along the former logging road that parallels Skunk Cabbage Creek conjures all manner of learning possibilities.

Consider that a redwood forest is not just a random collection of aged trees; rather, it is a repository of arboreal wisdom that, when experienced over time, can also be a lesson plan for life. Or, as forest philosopher Peter Wohlleben exclaims, "I will never stop learning from [trees], but even what I have learned so far under their leafy canopies exceeds anything I could have ever dreamed of."

Thus, on several of my redwood ventures I would locate a peaceful retreat beside a trail, in the midst of a cluster of ascending goliaths, or deep in the sanctity of a fern-filled glen. I would secure a position on a rustic bench or beside the weathered bark of a grand old tree and look around. Pen at the ready, my voice memo phone app poised, I would wait for inspiration. It didn't take long. In the notes that follow, I share with you one educator's lessons for a life well lived—lessons of longevity birthed by ancient beings experienced in environmental success.

Redwoods teach us patience. We live in a hurried world punctuated by fast food, quick downloads, and instant gratification. Our multitasked days are crammed with duties and responsibilities that crowd a perpetual "to do" list. Yet redwoods show us the value of an unhurried life. Redwoods become beautiful over time, year by patient year, century by patient century. Redwoods lead long lives because their ascent is measured and deliberate. The unhurried time they take to become full and complete reveals their grandeur.

Redwoods demonstrate tranquility. In the forest, there is surrounding peace. I find myself observing the little things in this ecosystem: the persistent stillness, dappled colors echoing off the leaves, the scamper of a small mammal or the measured bubbling of an adjacent stream. I've discovered features revealed by careful examination and patient observation. I am reminded that the world outside is filled with agendas and schedules. Yet, here is an opportunity to rediscover what is truly important; tranquility contributes more to an extended life than does the completion of a long list of obligations.

Redwoods show us our ancestry. In several encounters, I observed Gordian knots of intertwined roots, long sinuous tendrils that twisted and wrapped around the trees in a web of strength and support. Redwoods lack a long and anchoring taproot to stabilize them and hold them well into the ground. Rather, their roots create a matrix of support that helps them stand up to the strongest storms. In so doing, redwoods remind us of our own ancestry, of the heritage that anchors us and the family that secures who we are. Redwoods teach us that our family is often our strength. I am often reminded that we stand tall because of those who support us. Ancestors are like entwining redwood roots that embrace our lives with structure and clear purpose.

Redwoods show us strength. As a wise philosopher once said, "Life is tough!" With myriad forces impacting our lives, we may wonder how we will carry on. Redwood trees have a marvelous capacity to teach us to stand tall, to be proud of who we are and what we believe. Gazing upward into a canopy of redwoods, I suppose that redwoods show us how to grasp for the possibilities and soar past critics who moan, "It can't be done." Redwoods show us that no matter what our age or station in life there is always room—and reason—to grow.

Redwoods survive very well with a minimum of resources. Our lives are ones of accumulation. We gift our children with the latest educational software or creative playthings, presumably ensuring them an intellectual life full of joy and discovery. We present ourselves with the latest bling, biggest houses, chic clothing, and expensive wines from European vineyards. We are a nation of avid consumers. Redwoods, on the other hand, need little: an early morning carpet of coastal fog, an undulation of hills and snaky streams, and a persistence of sunshine throughout the seasons. None needs purchase; all are at hand. The simple life assures their longevity.

Redwoods show us the impact of interaction. One of the commanding themes of human longevity is the power of community. Compelling data demonstrates that when we humans work together to build strong and lasting communities there is both purpose and strength in our lives. In their cooperation, redwoods also create sovereign territories of protection and peace. Their mutual cooperation strengthens all. It is the power of the forest.

Redwoods teach us that we all have something to give. Just as young trees show both the wonder and power of new life, old trees sometimes tumble and fall. And, in their falling, they create wildlife sanctuaries, space for newly emerging sprouts, and a replenishment of the earth. Old trees are essential to the life of the forest, for, in truth, they renew it. In both life and death, redwoods share themselves. That is one of the great truths of the forest and one of the essential elements of nature. Cooperation, not competition, strengthens all. Giving back gives life to us as much as to our neighbors.

Redwoods bask in quiet. The world of redwoods is one of persistent escape: from the rush of traffic, overpowering details of an overflowing schedule, and electronic commitments that overwhelm our lives. Redwoods survive quite well in an environment that is both calm and unhurried. Their strength is in a world without clangs, clutter, or clamor.

Redwoods enhance their environment. Redwood trees leave it much better than when they arrived as tiny sprouts. They build arboreal communities, they enrich the soil as well as the air around, they absorb carbon and add immeasurable beauty to the area in which they live, and they hold the soil fast to the earth so that other organisms, both botanical as well as zoological, may benefit.

Redwoods, in their silent majesty, teach us that we are all stewards of the earth irrespective of whether we are silent titans soaring to the clouds or chattering humanoids trekking along needled trails in a northern California forest. Redwoods show us that ecological responsibility is a province of all living things.

Wise teachers, those redwoods.

CHAPTER 5

Kayaking through Time

Common name: Bald cypress
Scientific binomial: *Taxodium distichum*
Age: 2,628 years
Location: Black River, southeastern North Carolina

605 BCE, Pompeii, 151 Miles (243 km) South of Rome

A bank of dim stars hung overhead, the last remnants of a glorious night now changing into dawn. A flotilla of merchant ships tied up to an array of docks jutting out into the harbor told of a flourishing trade with countries throughout the wide expanse of the Mediterranean. On this morning, as on all mornings, small groups of young sailors, principally from seaside towns in Greece, stood patiently awaiting orders. Upon securing their gear and boarding their assigned vessels, they would slip out of the port to begin a seemingly unending series of long days climbing riggings, swabbing decks, repairing sails, cleaning latrines, and hauling freight in and out of dark holds. It was a difficult and demanding life, but one offering opportunity to experience new cultures and new vistas.

The magnificent town of Pompeii in the seventh century BCE stood on a coastal lava plateau overlooking the radiance of the

Mediterranean. The navigable Sarno River, flowing to the Bay of Naples, passed by this city of slightly more than ten thousand inhabitants. Initially constructed a century earlier, Pompeii was originally a loose congregation of five villages. The city's name, in fact, derives from Oscan, an extinct Indo-European language of southern Italy, and its word for the number five: *pompe.*

With the arrival of Greeks in and around 740 BCE, Pompeii became a city of Greek-style buildings, including the most important edifice of the time, a Doric temple built in or around 600 BCE. The structure, constructed primarily of the airy volcanic rock called tufa, had thirty-two wide-fluted sandstone columns, a series of broad high steps, and three separate altars. The temple was consecrated to the god Hercules, famous for his strength and numerous far-ranging adventures, the mythical founder of the city.

Thanks to its position on the western Italian coastline and its substantial presence as a major port of trade and commerce, Pompeii was a wealthy town, one of fine public buildings and luxurious private houses replete with colorful decorations, ornate furnishings, and exquisite works of art. Villas and vast estates bordered the city, highlighting architecture and lifestyles that distinguished the city as one of the most opulent in the country.

But unknown to the sailors who crowded the docks or the wealthy merchants who conducted their business in noisy taverns, there was an underground geological force brewing 10.1 miles (16.3 km) to the northwest. Mount Vesuvius, a conical volcano with a long history of explosive outbursts—there have been fifty-four confirmed eruptions during the last 11,700 years—was slowly building pressure. Less than seven hundred years later, Vesuvius would explode in a multiphase eruption, sending pyroclastic surges down its slopes. The intense volcanic flow ripped long-standing woodlands, primarily birch, from the soil. Trees of every dimension toppled as though matchsticks. Ash and cinders covered expanses of once-vibrant forests. None survived. Over two days the city of Pompeii also succumbed, entombed in an avalanche of tephra.

605 BCE, Eastern North Carolina

Before European explorers descended upon the continent, Native Americans traded freely with each other through complex political societies that respected the land and the bounty it offered. This time, between 1000 BCE and 200 BCE, was known as the Early Woodland period. In what was to become the eastern United States, some 4,843 miles (7,794 km) west of that great Greco-Roman city, Indigenous people engaged in rich and varied agriculture, transporting goods along extensive trade routes that led to the Great Lakes and the Mississippi River valley.

Many settlements rose along the eastern seaboard, primarily beside rivers and coastal lakes. In the surrounding lands, Indigenous peoples took advantage of food sources such as berries, nuts, grapes, and persimmons. Hunters fanned out across the landscape to hunt deer, beavers, bear, and raccoons. Numerous shell middens attested to the fact that inhabitants also took advantage of the rich bounty of the ocean, moving to coastal territories during the summer months when marine animals were plentiful and then moving to the interior during the winter to hunt.

The coastal geography included abundant clay, supporting a robust industry of pottery production. Pots were often elaborately decorations in a rich range of geometric patterns. The manufacturing process was rudimentary, with most pots constructed by hand rather than with a pottery wheel and used to transport food and other goods.

Men and women were each assigned specific responsibilities depending on location and time of year. This was an efficient society, one well established and prosperous long before the Roman Empire began its march across the European continent. It was onto this land that a tiny seed fell to the ground. Fortuitously lodged between clumps of swampy mud, it began a long process of growth.

In a distant time it would become legend.

Present Day

I dip my paddle into dark waters of the Black River, an approximately sixty-mile (96.5 km) tributary of the Cape Fear River in southeastern North Carolina. I pull forward, deftly switch over to my right-hand side, dip that end into the water, and pull again. I have done this many times in my visits to lakes and rivers scattered throughout Pennsylvania. On camping excursions and day trips to remote sections of the state, my kayak is essential. Long days on languid lakes or slow-moving streams are a reconnection and revitalization of my core. These are journeys of both biology and contemplation.

This day I am traveling with Don Harty, the general manager and owner of Mahanaim Adventures in Wilmington, North Carolina. An accomplished kayaker, Harty is leading me into the sanctity of Three Sisters Swamp to see some of the longest-lived trees on the planet.

The Black River gets its name from the dark waters along its course. Tannins, naturally occurring chemicals extant throughout the plant kingdom, infuse the stream. Wood, bark, rhizomes, roots, and even fruits all contain these antioxidants, which help preserve tissues against cellular aging. These powerful agents also stave off pathogens such as fungi, viruses, and bacteria, even when a plant is submerged in water. When trees die or topple into rivers and subsequently decompose, those tannins, over time, eventually leach into the water, giving it a characteristic dark appearance.

As we set out, a low bank of swirling clouds obscured the sun. There were predictions of rain for later in the day, but for now, the weather was a pleasant mix of humid air and warming temperatures. A lone wood duck comfortably reposed on a log watched our departure with indifference. Our paddles rhythmically dipped in and out of tranquil waters. The river meanders, its speed measured not in miles per hour, but in its patient passage between long reaches of bald cypress trees that have prospered along these banks for thousands of years. Don informed me that the river drops only about twenty feet (6 m) from its origin in southern Sampson County, North Carolina, on its sixty-mile (96.5 km) journey downstream to where it empties into the Cape Fear River fourteen miles (23 km) above Wilmington. On this river, placidity is more common than flow.

In 1994, the North Carolina Division of Parks and Recreation named the Black River a North Carolina Outstanding Water Source, a designation given only to the cleanest of waterways. As a result, it has become a popular location for recreational activities such as kayaking and canoeing.

We paddled slowly. There was no hurry. Tranquility pervaded the atmosphere, trees filled the spaces, and the journey continued past historical sites hidden among the underbrush. Along the left side of a rising bank visitors have discovered centuries-old pottery shards, remnants of the loose-knit tribes of Native Americans who created informal alliances along the river during another century. We glide by, eyes fixed on the ever-increasing population of bald cypress that begin to appear downriver.

Most of us are familiar with evergreen conifers, trees that maintain their leaves throughout the seasons. In contrast, bald cypress are deciduous conifers. In the fall, their needlelike leaves turn orange, red, cinnamon, and yellow, eventually littering the river with brilliant colors and vibrant patterns. The name "bald cypress" results from the fact that they disperse their leaves so early in the season, leaving bare branches at their crowns. They are the dominant species here.

I rested for a moment, my paddle positioned on the coaming of the kayak. Just to my right a lone dragonfly with oversized eyes passed by, most likely looking for prey. Don informed me that dragonflies are our friends—lots of dragonflies means fewer biting deerflies. Much earlier, I had doused myself with liberal amounts of bug spray. Nevertheless, I was thankful for any additional assistance from beneficial insects in the area.

The river began to narrow. River birch on the right displayed enormous balls of mistletoe among their branches. Two pileated woodpeckers danced branch to branch in an adjacent tree. As the water flowed around downed trees poking above the surface, the result of tropical storms or hurricanes, it created a kaleidoscope of light flashes over the surface, echoes of the sun occasionally peeking through overcast skies or the canopies of prominent trees.

After about a half-hour of paddling down the wide river, Don guided us into a small tributary. For the first time on our voyage, we saw an assembly of woody dwarfs poking through the surface of the water. It was a surrealistic scene in which the characteristic "knees" of bald cypress trees, the feature for which they are most famous, greeted us in abundance.

As the name would suggest, bald cypress knees appear like bent human appendages rising from the river. Bald cypresses typically grow in slow-moving bodies of water, most particularly in riparian expanses throughout the Southeast. Often scattered around the bases of these trees are clusters of these "limbs." Knees grow vertically from the roots, each with a near right-angle bend that eventually breaks the surface and, on average, achieving heights of approximately three feet (0.9 m). They are solid structures, but with centuries-old trees, internal rot can cause them to

Bald cypress "knees" are commonly seen poking through the placid waters of a meandering river.

become hollow over time. Indigenous peoples used these hollow knees as beehives.

Both mystery and scientific speculation surround cypress knees. The most common hypothesis about them is that because bald cypress trees grow in riverine environments or swampy conditions with low levels of dissolved oxygen, the knees, often referred to as "pneumatophores"—an aerial root specialized for gaseous exchange—function to transport air to underwater roots. This theory is based on the fact that all plants, including trees, require an air source in order for cellular respiration to take place. Some scientists, as well as several introductory botany textbooks, subscribe to the proposition that cypress knees are, quite simply, "breathing roots."

Another theory embraces cypress knees as a way of releasing methane gas from underground sources—an escape valve, so to speak. While methane is not toxic to plants, it doesn't have any noticeable benefits either. However, a research study on bald cypresses along the Ogeechee River in Georgia several years ago demonstrated that cypress knees produced a negligible amount (less than 1 percent) of methane emissions from the swamp, suggesting that this theory may be suspect.

Some botanists have proposed that knees serve as structures for anchoring a tree in an often-unstable substrate. This organic reinforcement would offer increased support for vulnerable trees, particularly in times of high winds or hurricanes. The added strength would ensure the viability and endurance of trees over centuries.

Another theory proposes knees as a method of catching nutrients as river water passes between them. As underwater "drift catchers," knees would accumulate microscopic organic materials during water movement and "hold" them until the tree eventually absorbed them. Unfortunately, there is insufficient data to confirm this supposition.

In the mid-1980s two scientists proposed that bald cypress trees used their knees as storage organs during times of environmental stress, such as droughts. Although amyloplasts, organelles that store starch, have been detected on the cut surfaces of knees, there is no confirmation that bald cypresses draw on those reserves when water levels are low or nonexistent.

With all this, it seems safe to say that after nearly two centuries of scientific research and deliberation there is no clear-cut answer for the function of cypress knees. They remain unexplained curiosities.

Farther down the river we heard the trill of birds. Aside from the dipping of paddles, it was the only sound. Don pointed out a parliament of barred owls hidden in a tree. This was a true wilderness of peace, calm, and abject tranquility. More cypress knees poke up from this dark tributary like silent sentinels, allowing us passage in and around but carefully guarding their domain.

Don related some of the river's history. "This used to be a river of commerce," he told me. "During the late 1800s to the early 1900s, scores of paddlewheel boats used to ply the Cape Fear River Basin, bringing supplies upriver for the people who lived along the banks. People living near the river would bring their goods to the paddlewheels and sell their wares." As Don told it, commerce was rich and vibrant throughout the basin for many years.

After an hour or so of paddling, Don notifies me that we are entering Three Sisters Swamp. I see no signs or markers. I trust my guide knows where he is. He tells me that the swamp comprises nearly three thousand acres (1,210 ha) managed by the Nature Conservancy in Bladen County. It is home to hundreds of ancient bald cypress trees, many of them more than one thousand years old. The swamp gets its name from three of the oldest trees that grow apart from each other. Genetic testing has determined that these three trees, though not side by side, are related. As we floated along, the surrounding trees became denser, the waters blacker, and the quiet more pervasive.

Curious as to how these trees reproduce in such a watery environment, I discover that like many trees (e.g., pine, birch, walnut, hazel) they are monoecious, producing both male and female flowers. Pollen from male flowers fertilizes female flowers, which in turn produce viable seeds. The male and female flowers develop in winter, and seeds result the following October and November. Then the seeds drop into a flowing river or in the runoff of autumn floods and float off to new locations. For one to three months they must remain in a swampy area or submerged in water. The constant moisture helps the seed coats swell and eventually soften. Although bald cypress seeds cannot germinate underwater, they can remain submerged for up to thirty months before germination. As the waters recede, the softened seeds become lodged in the soft soil along the river banks. They are then able to sprout and grow.

Don pointed out how easy it is to get lost in this preserve with all its tributaries, offshoots, and rivulets. A profusion of minor streams that branch off in haphazard directions and the tangle of trees scattered throughout this domain can be confusing. Each year, at least a dozen times, locals rescue people who get disoriented, kayakers who think that this is just a river that goes from Point A to Point B. As Don said, "There are no markers here, no way to tell what's part of the main river and what's part of a tributary, so people lose their sense of direction." Curious, I asked him if he has ever been lost in the swamp. With a grin on his face, he told me, "I've never been lost! However, on occasion, I have been momentarily turned around."

We glided past two half-submerged logs. On each was a small cache of empty clamshells, neatly arranged in shallow depressions in the trunk. Don informed me that this was the work of river otters, which will often dive for freshwater clams, climb onto the logs with their bounty, pull the shells apart, and then consume their dinner. Small pockets of these shells turn up throughout the swamp, indications that this is a vibrant and sustaining ecosystem.

Then, about twenty yards in front of me, there stood one of the oldest tree specimens in the world: a less than imposing bald cypress that as of 2023 had attained the age of 2,629 years. Cored in 2018, it is scientifically identified as BLK227.

It is not the tallest tree in the swamp. Neither is it the largest. I could have easily missed it if not in the company of an expert guide and chronicler of this dense ecosystem. Nearing the base, I saw that an abundant shawl of dark-green moss covered it. Under the clouded sky its bark appeared light gray in sections, a turn from its characteristic cinnamon color. Slowly casting my eyes upward, I noted several burls along its ascending height. Burls are common among these trees, each one a growth in which the wood grain has produced a deformed protrusion or rounded outgrowth. Often they are the result of an injury, fungal infection, or some form of stress.

I reached out and caressed the rough and uneven bark of this seminal giant. My left hand glided over swatches of moss and open sections of bare bark. The kayak bumped against it, and I gently pushed it away for fear of causing any injury, however minor, to this long-lived tree. It has claimed its station for more than thirty-four of my lifetimes, so far be it for me to bring it harm in what may be its golden years.

I inched the kayak around the circumference. Don pointed out a small hole approximately 4.5 feet (1.38 m) above the water-line. This was the exact bore hole used to take the assessment of the tree, the spot where researchers determined its age and longevity. The hole, barely one-quarter inch (0.6 cm) across, was a miniscule trace of human intervention into its life, a small blemish marking massive centuries.

In my transit around the tree's circumference, I brushed through a few arcing sprigs, each sporting clusters of rounded seeds. Each seed was about the size of a walnut, with a jade-colored and spotted exterior. This senior citizen seemed still ready for reproduction.

After ten minutes of reverent admiration, we continued our glide down the river. We soon came upon another distinguished denizen of the swamp. Here stands another oldster, one also named Methuselah. This one leans slightly to the east, and a similarly thick blanket of moss drapes it around its base. Wide circles of knees and several small saplings poking their heads through the blackened surface complemented a healthy array of ascending branches and rich foliage.

In 1985, radiocarbon dating, and tree ring mapping determined that Methuselah, officially known as BLK69, dated to at

least 364 CE. That made it the oldest known tree in the swamp at
the time. Today it stands not as the oldest tree, but most certainly
one of the oldest trees along this vibrant waterway.

Later research revealed that its coring indicated that
two of the most severe droughts in its history coincided with
the Lost Colony and Jamestown settlements. Although it is
roughly one thousand years younger than its relative a half-mile
(0.8 km) north, it has borne witness to the adoption of Christian-
ity by Constantine the Great, the founding of the Mongol Empire
by Genghis Khan, the Louisiana Purchase, D-Day, and 9/11. It
has lived through history and created its own unique
historical record.

It was now late morning, and Don and I entered an expanding sector of the river. Once again, the waters were smooth and
glassy. An occasional chirrup broke the overwhelming silence
among the trees. It was tranquility to the power of ten, just as it
has been for the past thousand (and more) years. So too, was there
a complete absence of human intervention—no crushed beer cans,
empty potato chips bags, or plastic detritus.

After a short lunch, we continued our glide down the widening river. I was curious about its preservation, and Don told me
that Three Sisters Swamp is the largest area maintained by the
North Carolina Nature Conservancy, which has protected significant portions of the Black River since 1989. At present, the Conservancy, along with a range of state conservation agencies and the
North Carolina Coastal Land Trust, owns 17,960 acres (7,268 ha)
along the Black River and its tributaries, including Three
Sisters Swamp.

That preservation is critical to the life and longevity of
bald cypresses. As arboreal residents of the rivers and streams
that crisscross this blackwater system, they are essential miti-
gants of devastating floods, their roots preventing excessive
erosion. They also capture pollutants and curb their spread

throughout the region. The trees are also beneficial to a wide range of creatures, including various amphibians that use the swamp as a necessary breeding ground, waterfowl and raptors that build nests in hollow trunks or looming branches, and various fish that spawn in and around submerged logs. The trees are their protectors.

We continued paddling through an enclave of cypress knees, and our conversation turned to wildlife. Wild turkeys and bobcats are the most common animals in these parts. Don also told me about the rare rainbow snake, a three-to-four-foot (0.9–1.2 m) reptile that leads a most secretive life in the swamp. What makes this snake distinctive is that unlike the more common coral snake, which has colored bands that encircle it, the bands on a rainbow snake run down the length of its body from head to tail. It is nonvenomous, but I couldn't help but glance nervously around the cypress knees for rippling stripes of orange, black, and yellow.

I asked Don why we had not seen a single alligator during our journey. Having recently read a news story about a woman who fell into a Florida swamp and was promptly attacked by two of these most ancient beasts—alligators first appeared during the Oligocene epoch about thirty-seven million years ago—I had been certain we would encounter several along the way. Don explained that those classic swamp creatures are more abundant downriver, near the Atlantic shoreline, where it is considerably warmer.

The swamp and its ancient trees are not a domain of sentimentality and nostalgia, although I concluded our trip with a deep sense of gratitude at having seen this remote place and its inhabitants. It is not a return to the past, but a sanctuary for the present. It is a place removed from everyday consciousness, from trials or artificial prerogatives or uncomfortable stressors, primal and necessary.

Humans today live in the stark reality of the Anthropocene, an unfolding time of climate change, ecological degradation, and the political hubris of short-term financial gains at the expense of a denuded planet. We are a civilization on the brink and, quite often, we cannot see our way beyond tomorrow or the next century. The Black River and its embrace of the Three Sisters Swamp lends us cognizance not of limits, but of existence and communion with earth and sky and water.

Dendroclimatologist Valerie Trouet, in her captivating book *Tree Story*, refers to the enigmatic bald cypress. She notes that these swamp dwellers often grow to heights of 150 feet (46 m) and diameters of twelve feet (3.65 m). Dating these trees, according to Trouet, often requires individuals to ascend the trees with climbing spikes, which, although they dig into the bark, do not harm the tree. Using a system of ropes and lanyards, scientists can then secure themselves above the tree's knees. There they position an increment borer in a thick portion of the trunk, easily penetrate the soft wood, and extract a thin core of wood for counting.

Trouet emphasizes that despite the wet conditions in which bald cypress grow, they are good recorders of change in the level of swamp water. She notes that when water levels are high, the trees enjoy good water quality with high levels of dissolved oxygen and nutrients. Their narrow tree rings reflect times when water levels are low and water quality is poor. Unsurprisingly, tree ring chronology offers a portal into the longevity of the species.

An article, "Longevity, Climate Sensitivity, and Conservation Status of Wetland Trees at Black River, North Carolina," appeared in a 2019 issue of *Environmental Research Communications*.

Among its revelations was the discovery of a certain bald cypress tree (BLK227) at least 2,624 years old (in 2019) along the Black River of North Carolina. Equally astounding was the announcement by the article's authors that the tree's age made it the oldest known living tree in eastern North America; the fifth oldest known continuously living, sexually reproducing, nonclonal tree species; and the oldest known wetland tree species in the world. Significant, too, was the announcement that another tree (BLK69), in the same general area, was cored and dated to be at least 2,088 years old.

The authors noted that because they had cored and dated only 110 living bald cypress at this site, which is a small fraction of the tens of thousands of trees still present in these wetlands, there could be several additional individual bald cypresses over two thousand years old along the sixty-mile (96.5 km) reach of the Black River. The announcement of the 2,624-year-old bald cypress (BLK227) also extended scientists' knowledge about ancient climates in the Black River region by an additional 970 years.

The researchers made a plea for preserving the trees, noting that massive tracts of the ancient bald cypress trees are virtually unprotected and in need of urgent conservation. As such, they are subject to the persistent encroachment of commercial development and the onslaught of environmentally suffocating tracts of new housing. Sometimes, however, select species benefit from a little human intervention in the form of a dedicated organization or a dogged individual, such as the Ancient Bald Cypress Consortium and David Stahle.

Stahle is distinguished professor of geosciences at the University of Arkansas and was the lead author of the paper on the discovery of the 2,624-year-old cypress tree (BLK227). Since 1980, he has directed the Tree-Ring Laboratory (TRL) at the University. The TRL, established in 1979, concentrates on the development of exactly dated annual ring-width chronologies from ancient forests worldwide. Their specialization is in the reconstruction of past climate and stream flow, the socioeconomic impacts of past climatic extremes, the dating of historic structures, and the identification and mapping of ancient forests. The laboratory is also active in the conservation of ancient forests and has assisted the preservation of old growth remnants in the cypress-tupelo forests of the South, the oak-hickory forests of the central United States, the blue oak and conifer woodlands of California, and the conifer forests of Mexico.

The Ancient Bald Cypress Consortium grew out of the work at the Tree-Ring Laboratory in an attempt, as Stahle put it, to help protect nature by conducting research in collaboration with colleagues in academia, land management, conservation, and the general public. It was increasingly evident that heavy logging, land clearing, encroaching developments, and human intervention, in all its various permutations, was having a negative impact on the sustainability of ancient bald cypress trees. Thus the consortium.

I caught up with Stahle in early spring while he was vacationing in Colorado. It was a semester's worth of insight in a single conversation. Initially, I was curious about how the bald cypress trees of the Black River have advanced our concept of longevity. Stahle explained that it has been known since the early twentieth century that bald cypress, particularly those in the Carolinas, could reach ages of a thousand years or more. Based on the work of Wilbur Mattoon, a forest examiner in the early days of the USDA Forest Service, scientists made tree ring counts on cut cypress logs. Mattoon visited industrial logging operations throughout the Southeast and spent a great deal of time counting tree rings. Stahle refers to this early research as the "signal work" on the longevity of bald cypress. Consequently, we have known since the early 1900s that cypress trees typically experience extended lives, often longer than a thousand years.

In the 1980s Stahle began field sampling in the Carolinas. At that time, the oldest bald cypress they could conclusively date with dendrochronology was 1,650 years old. Thinking that these trees were remarkably old, and that their age had not been well documented, Stahle and his colleagues returned to the Black River to do some concentrated research on the precise dendrochronological age of the trees. At the outset, the researchers knew that some trees do not form rings each year and thus have missing rings. Stahle informed me that the beauty of the bald cypress, in spite of its wetland habitat, is the very strong climate signal embedded in the growth rings and imprinted on the width of the annual rings. He went on to say that there is a positive and highly significant correlation between the ring-width chronologies of bald cypress and growing season precipitation. That is, the more precipitation there is from March until July, the fatter the tree rings are in spite of the frequent flooded conditions along the river.

He elaborated that this process involves evapotranspiration demand, the process by which water moves from the land to the atmosphere by evaporation from the soil and other surfaces and by transpiration from plants, and it is often so great that the trees cannot keep up and the root systems rise near the surface waters of the swamp. Consequently, during droughts, the root systems are exposed to the dry air, and the trees experience internal moisture stress. He went on to emphasize that scientists have identified climate response, that positive correlation with precipitation, in every single bald cypress chronology developed in the United States, Mexico, and Guatemala. And so, because of that strong imprint of climate, the growth rings can be cross-matched among trees, inconsistencies can be worked out, and a valid master chronology of tree growth can be developed for bald cypress going back thousands of years.

Their study proved that with dendrochronology and radiocarbon dating, some individual trees have lived for more than two thousand years at the Black River Preserve and some, according to the authors, most likely have lived for more than three thousand years. Stahle emphasized, "That's a bit of a revelation for the eastern United States." With the publication of the paper, Stahle and his colleagues held a press conference at the Nature Conservancy Black River Preserve to publicize the results. They also wanted to promote the reserve, increase interest in the trees, and raise money. Subsequently, they were able to raise significant funds as a direct result of the publicity surrounding the article's publication. They used those funds to acquire more property and better preserve the ancient cypress along the Black River.

My curiosity was piqued. Like any good college professor, Stahle had prompted a rash of questions. I wanted to know what ensured the longevity of these most distinctive trees.

"Bald cypress are genetically programmed to live a long time," Stahle explained. "They've evolved over geologic time and adapted to the conditions in their environment and those adaptations are encoded in their genome and passed on to the succeeding generation. This is true of all old-lived trees regardless of where they're found."

He went on to explain that one of the characteristic adaptations bald cypress have made is their incredible resistance to rot. Although they inhabit humid and moist environmental conditions, their longevity is highly dependent on their defiance of decay and decomposition. Stahle also emphasized another considerable factor in the environmental success of these valiant trees. That is, whenever hurricanes or high winds rip away their canopy, they can regenerate or sprout new branchlets that can grow into a new canopy. This occurs after the canopy has been damaged or even completely destroyed.

His passion clearly escalated when he told me that the Black River harbored a remarkably open canopy of ancient cypress trees that land-falling hurricanes had battered over the millennia, yet they still inhabit a landscape that looks like a land lost from the Cretaceous, the age of dinosaurs. "There's old trees elsewhere in the United States, particularly the West . . . but they don't grow out of these incredibly beautiful black waters of the southeastern coastal plains." As we concluded our conversation, Stahle put an exclamation mark on the significance of his research when he reminded me that old-growth forests are not renewable on any kind of human timeframe.

I ended the call and sat back in my chair, contemplating Stahle's words and their universal implication. Nature still has many secrets. Scientists often disappear beneath the fringes of its knowledge, occasionally teasing out inner facts with extended patience. Clearly, nature does not reveal its confidences willingly. But time is on its side, a length of centuries and a breadth of millennia often beyond the comprehension of humans.

Somewhere in the distant reaches of my memory, I recalled something John Muir once said: "The clearest way into the Universe is through a forest wilderness." This would include, I am certain, the forest wilderness of a slow and swampy river in southeastern North Carolina.

Gordon Hempton, in his compelling and insightful book *One Square Inch of Silence*, notes that quiet has become an endangered species. "Our daily lives," laments Hempton, "are overrun by a cacophony of human noise intrusions." Hempton took a cross-country road trip from west to east to record the natural voices of the American landscape before the soul-soothing terrestrial soundscapes vanish completely in the ever-rising din of human noise. In his journey, he recorded bugling elk, trilling thrushes, drumming prairie chickens, fluttering butterfly wings, booming waterfalls, the whispering of a floating leaf, and the soft cooing of a coyote pup. He says, "I'd rather listen than speak. Listening is a wordless process of receiving honest impressions."

In my journey along the Black River, I would occasionally pause at various places through the majesty of this environment. At times, it seemed as though the trees were a natural quieting agent. Their presence all around was a barrier to the intrusion of human noise that we all too often take for granted.

As I paddled around downed branches, across the acreage of a looming forest, and through these ancient organisms, I felt a hush all around. I also discovered a personal peace: a lowering of blood pressure, a physiological calmness, and a more tempered mind. I was well aware that sound pollution often triggers a negative response. As a result, one of its major health effects is chronic stress and high levels of stress hormones. This, as you might imagine, has a negative impact on human longevity. In this more tempered environment, we have an opportunity to relax and return to an evolutionarily more natural state.

Rivers flow through our lives, our expressions, and our history as does no other geographical feature. It has been estimated that the United States has more than 250,000 rivers, totaling more than 3.5 million miles (5.6 million km), a distance equivalent to approximately 141 circumnavigations of Earth or nearly seven times the distance from Earth to the Moon. So, too, are rivers critical markers of our culture and connection with nature. They crisscross the country, defining boundaries both real and political, providing nourishment and nutrients for a diversity of farms and agricultural endeavors, and offering myriad recreational opportunities from fishing to water skiing. We vacation on rivers, create our cities on rivers, and take advantage of their capacity to deliver large quantities of water to parched lands and vital reservoirs. So, too, do rivers create ecosystems, devastate croplands, move soil, and build habitats.

Kayaking among the ancient bald cypresses of the Black River alerted my senses and expanded my consciousness about the power and potential of the natural world. I was inspired to listen to what I should rather than to what I must endure.

CHAPTER 6

Beyond Memory

Common name: Quaking aspen
Scientific binomial: *Populus tremuloides*
Age: Between 8,000 and 12,000 years
Location: Fish Lake, Utah

~7000 BCE, Ontario Province, Canada

The wind, pregnant with ice crystals, whipped through the canyon as it had for thousands of years. Winter was approaching, and ice covered the river from bank to bank. The hills beyond, wrapped with a gossamer layer of snow, demonstrated the stillness that often accompanies the turn of seasons. Spreading forests of pines, cedars and spruces were commonplace. The waxy coating on their needles not only prevented them from losing water during the summer months, but also allowed them to survive the frigid conditions of winter; a time when temperatures spiraled downward and long bands of creatures began migrations to southern climes. The herd of mammoths stood in silence.

There were nine members: three juveniles and six adults, including their leader, a thirty-seven-year-old female who had made this trek every year since her birth. Having arrived less than forty-eight hours earlier, the herd had already suffered a tragedy: the death of its youngest member. One of the juveniles, in its quest to explore the terrain, had wandered onto a section of river with ice insufficient even for the weight of one infant. The youngster broke through and was trapped in the frigid waters. There was nothing its mother could do but stand on the shore as the newborn flailed and cried. He would soon succumb to the cold and drown.

Their kind had inhabited the wide tundra and glacial plains for millennia; woolly mammoths lived from the Pliocene epoch (from around five million years ago) into the Holocene (the current geological epoch, beginning about 11,700 years ago). Various species existed in Africa, Europe, Asia, and North America until their eventual extinction. Scientists long assumed that woolly mammoths became extinct about ten thousand to twelve thousand years ago. However, recent eDNA research of sediments indicates mammoths survived in north central Siberia at least as late as 2000 BCE, in continental northeast Siberia until at least 5300 BCE, and until at least 6600 BCE in North America. Their behavior and size were equivalent to that of a modern-day African elephant. Their sweeping and distinctive tusks were replaced six times during an individual's lifetime. Those ivories, often reaching lengths of ten to thirteen feet, were fearsome indexes of a formidable creature.

The matriarch stirred. Raising her trunk high into the air, she let out an emphatic shriek—a signal to move on. At the same instance, shadows moved through the trees beyond; creeping on padded paws, carefully and silently observing the potential food source. As the mammoths moved, so did the predators. The carnivores had not eaten in well over a week, and they desperately needed sustenance for themselves and their young. With an ailing oldster firmly in sight, they slunk ever closer. The valley was still. But not for long.

~7000 BCE, Central Utah

Long arcing plateaus and statuesque mountain ranges dominated the landscape some 1,900 miles (3,060 km) to the southwest of the Canadian canyon. The ever-present ice that blanketed this geology resulted in a dearth of vegetation. Beneath, the landscape was a potpourri of sedimentary, igneous, and metamorphic rocks along with more than five hundred minerals. It was a dynamic land, subject to earthquakes, volcanoes, landslides, floods, and other geological forces spread across four billion years. Also sculpted by glaciers and the subtle imprint of erosion, rocks folded and faulted, buckled and bent, and changed into vast conglomerates that were, at once, magnificent, and later, gone.

Human footprints crossed this land at least ten thousand years ago, during the Pleistocene. These nomadic people, traveling in small family groups, followed herds of woolly mammoths and bison and captured rabbits and ducks. A menagerie of megafauna, including giant sloths, camels, and now-extinct horses, also populated this land.

Around 9700 BCE the climate slowly shifted and changed. A once-frigid environment became a little warmer, a little dryer. Animals that could not adapt died off, as did plants that couldn't acclimate. Changes in the zoology and botany of the area also forced changes in the lifestyles of the Paleo-Americans who inhabited the region. Their tools changed, their lifestyles altered, and their customs modified. It was a slow, evolutionary process dictated by unseen forces in a changing environment. Central Utah was in flux.

Even so, a vast sheet of ice stretched beyond the horizon. Although it was slowly receding from south to north, its influence was omnipresent. Botanical life was scant, with not a tree to be found anywhere. As the ice retreated, it left behind a rough and scarred terrain. Broad lakes, eroded mountains, and a gorged geography of rounded hills and alluvial sediments were the remnants of its existence.

Present Day

I am going to introduce you to a single tree. It is solitary, and so it
rightly belongs in the next section of this book, which focuses on
individual specimens. I write of it here for two reasons, neither one
strictly scientific. First, most visitors see Pando (the tree's name)
as a collection of tens of thousands of "trees," an assembly not
unlike a collection (or forest) of oaks, pines, or elms in their
backyard or a local park. Second, there was a grammatical issue.
Yes, Pando is a single tree and has a singular name. But most
people refer to this giant clone in the plural: "Look at all these
beautiful aspen trees!"

In pursuing the wisdom of ancient woods, I heard tales
about an enormous tree lodged against the broadsides of a sweeping basin in south-central Utah. This organism defied human
expectations about size and mass and weight with parameters
seemingly beyond comprehension.

For a moment, consider the blue whale. This leviathan of the
sea gives meaning to the terms "enormous" and "gargantuan."
Reaching a maximum confirmed length of ninety-eight feet (30 m)
and an overall weight of 196 tons (177,808 kg), it is the largest
animal known to have ever existed. It is bigger than any Cretaceous sauropod or present-day terrestrial creature.

But it is no match for one well-lived plant in the canyonlands
of the westernmost Colorado Plateau. Genetic testing in 2008
confirmed the tree's enormous size: it spans 106 acres (42.9 ha),
the equivalent of sixty professional soccer fields placed side by
side. It has lived for approximately eight to twelve millennia, since
before the invention of the wheel, the creation of clay pots, or the
origination of metallurgy, and it tips the scales at an estimated
weight of 13.3 million pounds (6,032,779 kg), the heft of thirty-four
blue whales. It is massive, three times greater than the next largest
tree in the world, the General Sherman in Sequoia National Park.

Pando (Latin for "I spread") is an aspen tree, specifically a quaking aspen. Commonly associated with western North America, aspens grow at elevations from five thousand to twelve thousand feet (1,525–3,658 m). Known as a "pioneer species," they are often the first trees to germinate in locations where long-lasting glaciers, occasional mudslides, or severe droughts have swabbed the landscape. Frequently, they take root in the aftermath of a rampant wildfire.

A quick glance at this enormous organism seems as though you might be looking at a forest of more than 45,000 individual trees. In a sense, you are. But, like all aspen, Pando reproduces primarily by root sprouts—often known as vegetative regeneration or suckering. (Although botanically incorrect, common vernacular often refers to the mature growths, the vertical extensions, as "trees," "stems," or "suckers." For scientific accuracy throughout this chapter, I will use the more acceptable "branches.")

Aspen groves always originate from a single seedling. However, the rhizomatic nature, that is, the growth of a somewhat elongated, usually horizontal, subterranean plant stem, of that seedling's root system means that new shoots, or "suckers" correctly used, spring forth from the tree's long lateral roots. Those suckers grow vertically and are often mistaken for individual trees. They are, in fact, extensions of an often-complex web of roots entangled beneath the soil. In truth, a "grove" of aspen trees is a single tree with many skyward branches above the ground and a massive subterranean system tucked below the surface. This entire aggregation is commonly known as a "clone," a scientific designation for a complex of genetically identical individuals with similar characteristics and a common root structure.

Pando is thus a single organism, a male tree with more than 45,000 branches throughout its acreage. Each of those appendages can reach a height of eighty feet (24 m), a width of three feet

(0.9 m), and a mature crown of about thirty feet (27 m) in diameter. Although clonal, it's still an incredibly substantial tree.

An aerial photographer discovered Pando in 1976. Every branch of Pando is genetically identical, and in the fall, when leaves turn color, every one of Pando's more than 45,000 branches have the exact same blaze of color. From above, those colors clearly stand apart from the leaf colors of adjoining aspen clones. In essence, Pando outlines itself in bold relief from other aspen spreads with its own unique colors, pigments, or tones.

Though broad and expansive, Pando's singular distinction is not its size but its age. Or more precisely, a common misrepresentation of its age.

Once misinformation gets started, it becomes difficult to dislodge from the public consciousness. When this misinformation proliferates, via social media, for example, it quite often becomes fact. This is so even with plants. For example, there is a persistent claim that Pando is eighty thousand years old. The scientific reality is that Pando is not eighty thousand years old—not even close.

Strange to say, but the commonly reported age of eighty thousand years most likely originated in an undated US Forest Service document issued many years ago. Unfortunately, that figure was unaccompanied by original source material, a scientific footnote, or any verifiable research studies. It was, most assuredly, someone's guesstimate. Because the number appeared in a seemingly accurate resource, a rash of unverified journalism has repeated it uncritically. Authors of subsequent articles about Pando continue to repeat that number as fact, since it has appeared so many times previously, a "fact" without validation, scientific authentication, or peer-reviewed research.

That oft-quoted number is incorrect for several reasons. First of all, eighty thousand years ago the region we now know as south-central Utah was in the grip of a massive and persistent ice age. By definition, an ice age is an extended span of time, often millions or even tens of millions of years, when global temperatures are relatively cold and glaciers and enormous continental ice sheets veil large areas of Earth. Furthermore, ice ages are also divided into short periods of time (approximately ten thousand years each) that include warm temperatures, known as interglacials or interglacial cycles when glaciers retreat toward the North Pole, and colder temperatures known as glacials or glacial cycles when glaciers advance southward.

Throughout its history, Earth has experienced at least five major ice ages. The earliest was more than two billion years ago. The most recent period of expansive glaciation was the Laurentide Ice Sheet—the principle glacial cover of North America during the Pleistocene epoch (about 2,600,000 to 11,700 years ago). At its maximum extent, it spread as far south as latitude 37° N (roughly today's Utah/Arizona, Colorado/New Mexico, Kansas/Oklahoma borders) and covered an area of more than five million square miles (12,949,941 sq km), slightly less than the size of Antarctica today. At that time the world was, on average, between ten and forty degrees Fahrenheit (5.5 to 22° Celsius) colder than today. In short, what we now know as Utah was a bleak and frigid environment, one of plummeting temperatures and prodigious glaciers that sheathed large portions of the land. Those glaciers obstructed the germination and growth of most forms of plant life, including trees. In sum, eighty thousand years ago, much of the Northern Hemisphere (including present-day Utah) was a glacial void.

Second, it is difficult, if not impossible, to reliably calculate Pando's age. Because Pando is a single tree that encompasses an enormous area, determining a specific location within that specimen to conduct a tree-ring analysis would be akin to search-ing for the proverbial needle in the haystack. Each of its more than 45,000 branches is no more than about 150 years old, the maxi-mum life expectancy for an individual aspen branch, so they wouldn't be candidates for increment boring. Pando lacks the thick wood of redwoods or sequoias, making it virtually impossible to count rings beyond the life span of a single branch. The roots, because of their extensive and expansive underground lengths, would also be challenging to accurately date.

Radiocarbon testing, often used to date ancient objects, would also be difficult, if not insufficient for dating Pando. To do so, it would be necessary to discover a shard of one of Pando's stems from several thousand years ago. That relic would then allow appropriate testing. Unfortunately, though, scientists have not discovered any ancient remnants. Much of that challenge revolves around the question of where to even begin looking for an ancient fragment of Pando, particularly across an expanse of 106 acres.

As a result, there is no way to precisely test Pando's age using current technology. However, what scientists can agree on, at least as of this writing, is that the overall age of Pando can be no more than twelve thousand years. This is roughly the begin-ning of the last interglacial period. By the same token, the minimum age of Pando, eight thousand years, can be determined by the fact that an aspen clone spreads outward at a rate of approximately three feet (0.9 m) per year. Thus, by dividing the overall size of Pando by its estimated growth rate, we get a figure close to eight thousand years. Of course, this assumed growth rate is based predominantly on ideal environmental conditions for Pando's growth: persistent sunlight and lots of moisture from rain and melting snow. Consequently, a scientific estimate of eight thousand to twelve thousand years old seems to be the most appropriate bracketing and most reasonable estimation of Pando's overall age.

As an environmental organization, Friends of Pando is a formal association of scientists, forest service personnel, botanists, arborists, environmentalists, ecologists, high school and college students, and everyday citizens who have a passion for Pando and a desire to learn more about its secrets. This group is deeply concerned with preservation issues and the ways in which Pando can survive for thousands more years. Their mission is to promote awareness of Pando, ensure its survival, and dispel numerous false claims.

The executive director of Friends of Pando, Lance Oditt, fell in love with trees in his youth. His first encounter with Pando was in 2017, and by 2019 he was organizing calls with people who also shared his passion for the tree and wanted to ensure that generations to come could enjoy this natural wonder. With a background in public service, in concert with multiple experiences leading large-scale projects in the high-tech sector, his position as executive director offers opportunity to blend art and science to inspire stewardship and long-term thinking about preserving this quintessential tree.

I came to understand Oditt's passion for this specimen over several phone calls and Zoom meetings. Conversations were like discussing a classic World Series game with an old friend over a couple of beers at the local pub. He was self-effacing, gregarious, and downright informative. He is clearly in love with this tree, his responses to my questions passionately demonstrated his commitment to a most uncommon plant. "People should visit Pando because we live in a world where Pando is possible. You don't have to have an environmental mindset or be a scientist to appreciate Pando. You can just be with the tree," he told me.

Oditt explained to me that even though Pando is the largest aspen, heaviest tree by weight, and the largest tree by weight and land mass, what seems to attract people most is that Pando redefines what a tree can be by the mere fact that it is what it is: a single tree comprising more than 45,000 genetically identical branches connected by a root system that balances energy production, defense, and regeneration across a huge tract of land. Said Oditt, "You can't just think like a botanist, geologist, ecologist, or land manager when thinking about Pando: it demands an interdisciplinary approach; a redefinition of 'tree-ness.'"

I was curious about what Pando could teach us about longevity. Oditt was effusive when he recounted his first visit to the behemoth. At that time, he focused his attention on the struggles of the tree as they were understood at the time and was receptive to influences and other people's ideas about Pando. Later, having spent considerable time inside the tree, he realized that Pando was reinventing itself despite botanical stress and challenges—in fact, in response to it. As he explained, if you cut a branch off Pando, the tree will typically send up a new branch from the root to rebalance the system. When that happens, the latticework of roots that secure the ground upon which it stands, expands, hence the name Pando. The sight of this set of branches reminds me that as vertical appendages, branches may appear along the entire root structure of an aspen. Each branch is capable of living for approximately 150 years, but the root system may have a life expectancy of several thousand years. In Pando's case, that system is huge: Paul Rogers, director of the Western Aspen Alliance and chief scientist for Pando, has estimated that the tree's entire root system, if laid end-to-end, could conceivably extend for twelve thousand miles, or halfway around the planet.

I asked about the long-simmering controversy about Pando's age—specifically, the age so often misrepresented in the popular press, on internet web sites, in blogs and social media, and on posted videos. I asked Oditt how the figure of eighty thousand years old originated, and he replied that it was promoted early on as a guess, a date that we now know cannot be correct. Glaciers covered the land on which Pando grows and frigid weather patterns prevailed until approximately twelve thousand years ago, a significant factor that would have been inhospitable to any tree. He noted how people often get attached to the idea of extreme ages or simply large numbers, readily accepting forty thousand or even eighty thousand years, yielding a potential funding problem for a nonprofit: an extreme age can discourage financial investment and contributions because people will think that the tree is effectively immortal, so of no pressing concern. Regardless, Oditt continued, it does provide a most interesting lens about our human, frequently fictionalized ideas of longevity.

Oditt cautioned me that even though Pando is distinguished by an extended life, it also suffers from a constant battle with its nomenclature. He told me that a lot of academics, land managers, the media, or folks who reach out to Friends of Pando tell him that Pando should not be classified as the "largest tree" because it is a clone, something he finds to be quite strange. He makes the point that approaching Pando as an aspen clone can help us understand some of what we need to do to take care of it. But he also sees how insisting on the "clone" nomenclature has the opposite effect of getting anyone to care, which is a big problem when soliciting funding. He emphasized that with Pando we often get superlative headlines and boring codas. "The world's largest clone," he points out, is hardly engaging to a prospective donor.

Oditt went on to remind me that we have less than two decades of research on Pando. A lot of that data is actually based on generalized research about aspens and not Pando itself. As a

result, researchers make educated guesses that Pando has characteristics or features similar to other aspens. In some instances
that's accurate, in others perhaps not so much, if only because
Pando is so much larger a clone than its aspen kin.

By this point in our string of conversations, I was sufficiently
curious about the connection between Pando's history and its
future. Oditt's response was both candid and precise. "We now
have a long-term partnership between Friends of Pando and
Fishlake National Forest where we can work closely to explore
funding opportunities, preservation, programming, plans to
educate the public, while also taking care of the tree based on the
best research we have today—something that has never been
done with Pando. We are at the beginning of a story where we
know Pando is alive and we are alive in a world where Pando is
possible. Pando is an opportunity, on a small scale, to do big
things."

"In the end," Lance Oditt said, "Pando is a tree that is
constantly changing." I agree. Pando changes our concept of what
a tree can be as much as it changes our concept about the longevity of trees in general. After several conversations with one of its
protectors, it was time for me to see it for myself.

Clouds hugged the horizon as our flight landed in Grand Junction,
Colorado. We exited the plane, obtained our luggage and a rental
car, and headed west on Highway 70 for the drive to Fish Lake,
Utah. As we passed over the Colorado/Utah border, the scenery
changed. Everywhere we looked were wide vistas of sienna and tan,
with a noted absence of green. Long rocky ridges, carved by the
wind, revealed a wonderland of geological designs and sculptures.
The highway took us just north of the iconic Arches, Canyonlands,
and Capital Reef National Parks. After a journey of three and a half

hours, we drove into the magnificent vistas of Fishlake National
Forest, the home of Pando.

Pando stands above six-mile (9.6 km)-long, one-mile (1.6 km)-
wide Fish Lake. Along with clusters of sagebrush and juniper, the
tree sits at an elevation of 8,848 feet (2,697 m), straddling both
sides of Utah Route 25. Many of the visitors Pando receives each
year are surprised to discover a major transportation artery
running through the heart of this beloved tree. In the early eigh-
teenth century, a leg of the Old Spanish Trail, a historical trade
route approximately seven hundred miles (1,125 km) long that
connected northern New Mexico settlements with those in southern California, crossed the area where Pando lives. In 1918, a road
from Plateau Junction east to Fish Lake joined the state highway
system. Numbered SR-25 by the state legislature in 1927, the west
end was eventually moved south to Fish Lake Junction in 1935 as a
federal aid project.

After we passed a sign signaling the perimeter of Pando, tall
aspen branches that crowded out other denizens of the landscape
embraced us. Tall fencing on both sides of the road protected the
branches. The fencing, erected in 1992, 2013, and 2014, protects
young aspen suckers, a food source for seasonal livestock and
wildlife that, quite often, do not have sufficient numbers of
natural predators to provide a check on their populations. Approximately fifty-three acres (21.4 ha) of the tree have been fenced to
protect it from more intensive browsing by deer and elk. Strategi-
cally placed gates around the perimeter, however, allow
human access.

Less than two miles (3.2 km) later we came upon Fish Lake
Resorts, where we planned to stay. I was able to make contact with
Lance Oditt, who had been on site for several months. He arrived
at our cabin, and we discussed some preliminary details for our
various excursions into Pando. Exhausted from a full day of travel,
we retired early.

I arose the next day at 5:30 a.m. and stood before the largest natural mountain lake in Utah, with the sun etching its way over smoothed mountains encircling this placid enclave. Firs and spruces spread their greenery across the valley. The rising sun echoed over their branches and swept across perimeters of the verdant valley.

Shortly before 10:00, Oditt and an assistant arrived to transport us to Pando. In less than five minutes, we squeezed ourselves through a gate and along a faint trail. Here the tree trunks were blazingly white, their crowns rustling in a light breeze. We had entered another world, another dimension.

Lance and I set out on an uphill hike to explore the rough and rugged terrain. Lance informed me that geologists call the basin a "graben," a valley with distinct escarpments on each side caused by the displacement of a block of land downward. Parallel normal faults often produce these escarpments, with the displacement of the hanging wall downward and that of the footwall upward. Rift valleys are often the result of a graben—or several of them. The deep valley in which Lake Tahoe lies is a well-known example of another North American graben.

As we wound our way between a profusion of low-lying juniper bushes, I asked Oditt about some of the misconceptions associated with Pando. He reiterated how Utah State Route 25 cut through the tree long before Pando was discovered. As a result, many people believe the road cut the tree in half, but there is no scientific data or interpretation to suggest that that is the case.

As we hiked, Oditt noted that the tree has survived three-hundred-year droughts, including environmental disasters that drove out many human inhabitants. I considered recent articles about the perilous aridification of large segments of the American Southwest due to insufficient rainfall and a reduced snowpack throughout western states and along the length of the Colorado

River, a terrestrial dehydration currently in its third decade. How would Pando survive this current calamity, I wondered.

Oditt was most demonstrative when he tackled the topic of science communication or, more specifically, how the internet precipitates a wealth of misinformation and invented anecdotes about Pando's health. Many postings embrace the supposition that Pando is dying. He told me that there is no clear evidence of that. "We know that it is struggling to regenerate, but we don't have a set regeneration rate—that's still an unknown. The problem is that when people say that something is dying, they are often talking about something that will be gone. That drives a disaster mentality. It also drives helplessness: there's nothing that can be done to save the tree, when that is simply not the case."

We continued our hike up and over a profusion of boulders and open patches of scruff and between majestic stands of Pando's branches. Occasional squirrels darting over fallen logs were our only companions. Climbing higher, I recalled that Pando, like all aspens, is a deciduous tree. The characteristically mottled white bark contrasts with the various shades of brown common to the conifers that dominate mountainous terrains. In actuality, aspens' smooth white bark is sometimes tinged with shades of green, yellow, or gray. Interestingly, they are also unique in having chlorophyll in their bark, so that not only do their leaves photosynthesize but so does their bark, something aspens are able to do during the decidedly chilly days of winter to keep the sap flowing.

Also distinctive about aspens is a congregation of "eyes" scattered across the bark. These oval-shaped scars resemble the outlines of human eyes, quite a surrealistic vision when hiking through an aspen forest. The eyes are places where horizontal branches fall off as the vertical branches grow upward. The absence of those woody extensions close to the ground prevents forest fires from ascending up into the crowns, which would

The "eyes" of an aspen tree indicate that once-living branches
have separated from it.

increase the intensity of a surrounding conflagration, ensuring
greater damage to the tree. Indeed, an aspen colony can successfully survive a devastating forest fire simply because its massive
root system lies well below the intense heat of a wildfire. Coinci-
dentally, aspens also provide natural fire breaks for low and
medium intensity fires as the wood has high water content, a
factor that mitigates any propensity for burning. After a fire burns
out, new aspen branches appear, and the tree continues its life.

Sucking air rarified at only 14.8 percent oxygen, we secured a
resting place on an oversized boulder lodged between a thick and
expansive stand of aspen branches. I asked Oditt the inevitable
question: Why has this particular aspen tree grown so large? He
answered that part of the reason Pando has gotten so large owes
primarily to its adaptations. He pointed out that Pando is a stable
aspen clone, meaning it dominates the land and is able to withstand adverse conditions such as landslides, avalanches, earthquakes, and windstorms. Each time one of the branches goes
down, there is a hormonal response that sends a signal to the tree:
"Pando, get going, spread out." Anywhere there is a root, a new

branch can go up. As a result, every time something knocks something else out, Pando can take advantage of it. Oditt added, *"Populus tremuloides* is one of the fastest growing trees in North America and can grow up to three feet a year. So it's going to be hard for another tree to get going that fast and get into the sky before Pando does."

Oditt emphasized that Pando is alive, is vibrant, and is constantly regenerating, rebalancing food, resources, and defenses, all across a massive scale. When visitors arrive at the tree, they traverse an ancient and perpetual dynamic. He pointed out that Pando is a complex tapestry of robust ecological principles that underscore the idea that humans are a unique part of nature just as the tree is. The eyes up and down the trunk, the land's turbulent tectonic and volcanic past, fallen leaves that replenish and rebuild soil after summer monsoons, pale white bark that protects the tree from harmful UV rays, the complicated root network underground, and the countless opportunities for regeneration all highlight a complex strategy for life.

As we continued our hike, I recalled that aspens thrive in areas with abundant sunlight and are intolerant of shady ecosystems. Nevertheless, they can grow in a wide variety of soil types ranging from sandy or gravely substrates to rich, humus-laden environments. They require abundant water and are frequently located in riparian valleys and beside meandering streams. Over time, they have been able to adapt to a distinctive range of ecosystems and environmental challenges.

Any wisp of wind or subtle breeze reveals one of Pando's most distinctive characteristics—their trembling or quaking leaves, which gives the aspen its "tremulous" name. Aspen leaves are unique. Each leaf is thin, firm, and almost round. They are pointed at the apex and rounded at the base with many sharply pointed teeth along their edges. Most distinguishing, however, is the flattened leaf petiole, or stem, which lies perpendicular to the leaf blade. The flattened stem is an aerodynamic feature that reduces drag on the branches and trunk, thus causing the leaves to quake or tremble in even the lightest breeze.

As to the future of Pando, Oditt told me that he had been coming out here for only six years, a tiny segment of the tree's life. He believes that Pando has some surprises in store over the next two hundred, five hundred, or one thousand years. "I get this feeling that this tree knows this land in a way it will take us a long time to catch up on," he said.

In our walk, I noted that several branches are dying, victims of an insidious disease that shortens their lives. Oditt replied that three diseases afflict aspens: sooty bark canker, leaf spot, and conk fungal infection, all of which affect the tree as well as its prodigious root system. Scientists are unclear about the severity or extent of these diseases and whether they are recent afflictions or whether Pando has battled them over the entirety of its life. Suffice it to say, the question merits careful observation.

Oditt reminded me that Pando is constantly changing, constantly evolving. In some places it pops up new growth; in other places, it struggles to survive. So, too, does it contend with a range of environmental challenges spawned by climate change—increased levels of atmospheric CO_2, extreme weather events, soil acidity, the greenhouse effect, and human intrusions. Over time, it has proven itself resilient. What awaits it in the future is less certain.

Walking through the majestic realm of Pando is cathartic. There is a presence of calm and peace that overrides artificial intrusions. I noticed that my pulse slowed and my tension had dissipated. My journey through the grandeur of Pando clearly underscored the Japanese practice of *shinrin-yoku*, or "forest bathing," simply retreating to a forest environment to experience it through all our senses. It is not an exercise, but rather a reconnection with nature. It is a more natural and normal existence where we have opportunity to take in the bend of branches, a flight of migrating birds, the scent of flowered meadows, the taste of a pungent breeze, or a palette of evening colors across the sky. We have an opportunity to reconnect and reorient with a more natural world.

Empirical research has demonstrated that sustained time in nature has a most positive effect on our health. A walk in the woods, a passage along a forest trail, a sojourn to a rustic lake or a quiet seashore, or a simple picnic in an urban park has many benefits. These include a reduction in blood pressure, lower stress levels, improved cardiovascular health, a boost in the immune system, lower blood-sugar levels, improved concentration, and weight reduction among others. Regular opportunities to engage with the natural world are one of the great tonics of our lives. It may also be a lesson in longevity. Breathing Pando was an injection of spirit, an infusion of purpose, and an embrace of wonder, all learned from an organism that has mastered the elements and survived. Quite well.

CHAPTER 7

Giants of the Sierras

Common name: Sequoia

Scientific binomial: *Sequoiadendron giganteum*

Age: ~3,200 years

Location: Sequoia National Park, Central California

1178 BCE, San Lorenzo Tenochtitlán, Veracruz, Mexico
Baba-Ku was a master craftsman, a stone carver of Olmec rulers whose reputation for precision was well known throughout the kingdom. Priests revered him and commoners celebrated him as an artist of remarkable talent, displaying his work at the temple in the middle of the settlement, the highest honor. The stone he carved came from the Tuxtla Mountains, a vast region of alluvial fans flush with basalt. Baba-Ku diligently handpicked his stones for quality and symmetry. He wanted only the best.

Each head was carved from a single basalt boulder. Those individual boulders may have been transported sixty miles (96.5 km) or more from its original location to the village. On land, log rollers from walnut trees, calote pines, or sapodilla, sturdy native trees 115–130 feet (35–40 m) tall, were most likely used to move the enormous rocks. It is speculated that river transportation of the boulders was carried out through the creation of grand balsa rafts, from balsa trees, also native to the region, which grow up to ninety feet (27.4 m) in height.

Over the years, Baba-Ku mastered his chisels with both precision and artistry. He knew the angles that worked and those that might lead to destruction. He learned to apply the right amount of pressure on each tool, mastery learned through years of both failure and success. For much of his work, sound determined whether he was progressing satisfactorily. Some sounds were rich; others were vacant. His success grew from the tone that echoed from each chisel strike.

Like many sculptors, Baba-Ku observed each rock from several angles. He would often return to a boulder over several months, scanning it from every conceivable orientation. In his charge to turn lifeless chunks of rock into the heads of designated rulers, visualization was critical. What he saw in his mind would be what he created from the stone. He believed that the boulder concealed that form, and that his chief pursuit would be to release it from its stony prison. So too, was he aware that the creation of a ruler's head was a reflection of the individual's experience, emotions, and soul. It had to be perfect.

Most sculptures took years to craft. No one set a time limit in which Baba-Ku had to finish carving his figures. While his assistants carved away major chunks of stone, only he could provide the subtle and precise cuts necessary for a masterpiece to emerge. Often, he began work on one rock only to discard it for another. The work was laborious and tedious. But Baba-Ku, unlike others, was persistent to a fault. His works, and the dignitaries he immortalized, would survive for centuries, long after his passing.

1178 BCE, Central California

1,820 miles (2,929 km) to the northwest of Veracruz, diverse Indigenous nations inhabited a rich and abundant ecosystem. These included the Washoe, Yokut, Nisenan, Central Pomo, Miwok, Ohlone, and Yana, all of whom took advantage of the abundant plant and animal life. Trade among these peoples was both common and necessary. Resources such as shells (used as a measure of currency), obsidian, salt, dried nuts, acorns, and alkali fly larva (used for a high-protein flour) were frequently exchanged. Tribes also traded fish, elk, squirrels, quail, antelope, turtles, mussels, pigeons, eels, clams, and rodents. Plants resources included clover, tule grass, Sierra plums, buckeye nuts, strawberries, wild grapes, blackberries, and wild honey.

These Indigenous tribes, primarily hunter-gatherers, also engaged in a practice that both preserved and enhanced the local environment. Known as "forest gardening," tribes used a form of controlled burning to prevent large, destructive fires. They burned underbrush and grasses systematically, rotating the burn sites. This revitalized wide swaths of land while encouraging the growth of new shoots to attract the variety of game that inhabited the region.

Their religion was animistic: the belief that all objects, most fervently natural objects, have spirits or souls. Those souls existed not only in humans, but equally so in rocks, plants, animals, and most assuredly, trees. Only recently have modern-day scientists discovered the underground communication networks that allow trees to send "signals" to one another about disease, drought, or insidious infestations of insects. It seems that ancient tribes intuited the "inner workings" of trees, characteristics now proven by research.

Around 3,200 years ago, after a periodic fire, a cone released a seed. Dropping to the ground, the seed lodged in the fertile soil and germinated, sprouted, and began to grow. Its nourishment and sustenance ensured by the topography, it prospered and rose—millimeter by millimeter, foot by foot—toward the warmth of the sun. Protected and sustained by others of its kind, it eventually became one of the oldest, and most respected, members of the planet. It was a sequoia tree, a botanical pillar revered by generations of Native Americans. So, too, would immigrants and travelers of another millennia come to stand in its shadow and gaze at its splendor.

Present Day

It was a husk, a charred and crippled skeleton of a once former giant. Its life extinguished, it still maintained its arborescent post as it had for centuries. But now consumed by one of nature's most misunderstood elements, it was a blackened shell. Encircling it was a density of ash and the equally charred remains of neighbors. The land was an unresponsive void that had been ravaged by an engulfing force that razed the land, consumed its inhabitants, and extinguished every living timber.

We parked in a short pull-off along General's Highway just to the east of Ash Peaks Ridge in Sequoia National Park. The late spring sun vibrated off the escarpments and mountain ridges before us. Yet, as we gazed down the slope, we saw once-tall sequoias obliterated by the ferociousness of the KNP Complex/Windy Fire of 2021. Acres of burned forest lay before us. Grand and regal trees had succumbed to an unimaginable devastation, one sparked not by incautious humans but rather by a natural constant of alpine environments: lightning.

Scanning the terrain before me, I breathed in short gasps. Trees that had dominated this slope for millennia, long before the intrusion of modern humans and the roads they built for logging enterprises and international visitors, had been seared beyond imagination. An expanse of charcoal skeletons littered the hillside, a graveyard of various species including sequoias. Estimates are that the two fires of 2021 consumed up to 5 percent of the world's total population of sequoia trees. Add in the 14 percent of the total sequoia population wiped out by the Castle Fire in 2020, and almost one-fifth of these regal and ancient trees burned to death in a span of less than two years. According to estimates, upward of 10,000 mature giant sequoias went up in flames during the Castle Fire of 2020. In 2021, approximately 2,400 sequoias burned to death in the KNP Complex Fire, and the Windy Fire incinerated 1,250 more.

Counterintuitively, fire is an essential element contributing to the long lives of these majestic trees. Long before the arrival of

European Americans, Native Americans realized the value of fire in the overall ecology of sequoia forests. Naturally occurring fires, often the result of lightning strikes, grilled areas with low intensity burning of the underbrush and the usual detritus of the forest. The sequoias thrived. In turn, this created better hunting, grazing, and living conditions for humans. So, too, did tribes manipulate forest cycles through a judicious use of prescribed fires at periodic intervals.

Yet European settlers saw fire as a destructive and violent element in the life of a forest and determined that forests should be protected at all costs. Thus, in the years between the 1860s and 1960s, fire suppression became the signature management tool for American forests. Unsurprisingly, during that period, many forests throughout the Sierra Nevada became overgrown with trees, shrubs, and bushes along with the usual array of downed and dead materials. This accumulation turned once thriving forests into tinderboxes. In turn, many of the natural processes essential to the life of a forest were seriously curtailed. Many forests became their own fire hazards.

With a thick and fibrous bark, sequoias have a natural insulation against the intense heat of a forest fire. As these giants ascend to enormous heights, they discard most of their lower branches. This naturally occurring process (similar to that of aspens) is a preventative measure that significantly hinders a fire from climbing up into the branches of a tree.

While sequoias have natural defenses against fires, fire is a significant and consequential part of a sequoia tree's propagation, specifically with seed dispersal. Like other conifers, sequoia seeds form inside seed cones near the top of the trees. The seed cones can mature in less than two years although they typically remain green and closed for up to twenty years. Each of the cones has between thirty and fifty spirally arranged scales, with several seeds on each scale. There is an overall average of about 230 seeds per cone. Each seed is 0.18 inch (0.46 cm) long and 0.04 inch (0.1 cm) broad, with two 0.04-inch "wings" on either side, approximately the size of a tomato seed. It takes about 91,000 of these seeds to add up to a pound.

Some seeds are released when the cone scales shrink, typically in late summer when the ambient temperature is hot. Most, however, are freed by insect damage or when the cone dries from the heat of an approaching fire. As a heated cone dries, it contracts and releases its seeds to fall to the forest floor. Most sequoias have as many as 11,000 cones and consequently disperse an estimated 300,000 to 400,000 seeds annually. The winged seeds may fly up to six hundred feet from the parent tree. They often find their way to the forest floor where bare soil, made available by the passage of previous fires, is available for germination. Those conflagrations, in their passage, remove old plants and forest litter, which in turn opens gaps for sunlight to enter, giving the seeds an ideal location to grow and prosper. Although sequoias produce hundreds of thousands of seeds, less than 1 percent will eventually germinate.

Tree rings offer up some valuable information about this process because tree ring samples often reveal the history of fire in a particular area. When fire scorches a tree, the tree gluts its wound with sap. This protects the wound from wood rot decay, often for several centuries, as long as forest fires keep burning at a low intensity. Scientists have noted that tree ring records (which may include a measurement of extruded sap) show that, over the past two thousand years, fires were regular ways in which the forest maintained itself. When the climate was moist and wet, fires were less common; during intense dry periods, fires increased in regularity. Rings demonstrate that nondestructive fires occurred regularly at intervals between six and thirty-five years before the mid-1800s.

After that time, fire frequency dramatically decreased. Three intersecting factors contributed: a reduction in the number of fires set by Native American tribes, a significant increase in sheep grazing that cleared out vegetation and debris from the forest floor, and, most important, active fire suppression by state and federal agencies.

Beginning in the 1970s, the Forest Service showcased the concept of prescribed burning as a fire management tool. According to a Forest Service document, "Prescribed fire is a planned fire ignited under optimal conditions by qualified park staff. Prescribed fire may be used to restore fire-dependent species, to create diverse habitats for plants and animals, or to reduce fuels and prevent a destructive fire. 'Fuels' include both live plants as well as dead plant materials like logs, sticks, and dry pine needles." These "official" fires, the document continues, "are purposely set under highly regulated conditions and managed within a planned, geographic area. Today, prescribed burning is still an essential part of how we manage sequoia groves in the park." Government workers plan, coordinate, and regulate these conflagrations—in short, humans controlling an ecosystem.

Talking with Valerie Trouet at the Laboratory of Tree-Ring Research at the University of Arizona, I was curious about the role of fire in the lives, and most specifically, the longevity of sequoias. She told me about a substantial sequoia slab at the Tree-Ring Lab that has at least one hundred fire scars. This indicates that fire is a constant in the lives of these giants and that the trees have been able to survive those conflagrations over the span of their lives, which typically exceed two thousand years. She noted this is the natural fire regime in the Sierra Nevada and emphasized that these are fires happen every five to ten years, burning off the undergrowth, the grasses, the brush, and small trees. They typically do not kill sequoias. They might hurt them. They might damage them. But they never get big enough to actually reach the crowns and kill the trees.

The Forest Service and other agencies and settlers suppressed those fires. That practice actually had a detrimental effect:

by putting out the fires that burned off the underbrush, the Forest Service let that fuel build up for about a century. The result of those actions is that there is so much fuel in the forest that these fires are no longer ground fires. They're enormous fires, like the ones in 2020 and 2021, that quite often reach the crowns of the trees— eventually destroying the entire organism.

"We're now in a whole other fire regime," Trouet remarked. A Sequoia National Park ranger underscored her point when he told me, "Sequoias are fire-resistant, but they're not fireproof."

On one long journey through the sequoias, my wife and I pulled into a picnic area set among a magnificent grove of towering trees. We ate our lunch surrounded by the beauty of giant trees all around. My wife would note a yellow warbler, or I would pick up the cascade of wind through ascending branches. Our senses were on full alert as a panoply of sights and sounds graced our meal. We talked about the longevity of these massive beings, how they had survived here for centuries. At the time, we posed unanswered questions: How had they endured all the usual forces that brought lesser trees down? What contributed to their long lives? Later research revealed that a class of astringent, polyphenolic biomolecules may be part of the answer.

Sequoias ensure their longevity through preservative chemicals known as tannins. First discovered in 1831, tannins flow through many species of plants (such as bald cypresses), where they are important in protecting those plants from predation from birds and insects. They may also help regulate plant growth. The astringency, or puckering feeling, you get while drinking coffee, tea, or red wine is from natural tannins in the beans, leaves, and grapes used to produce those beverages. Tannins infuse many of the foods we consume, including strawberries, pomegranates, cranberries, blueberries, certain kinds of nuts, various spices, red beans, chocolate, and the malt and hops used to manufacture some types of ales and lagers. Quite often, tannins leach out of plants and seep into ground water, streams, or lakes. The result, as with the waters of the Black River which we saw in chapter 5, is dark or tea-colored water.

Tannins are best known as an important ingredient in the process of tanning leather. Throughout history, tanbark from oak, mimosa, chestnut, and quebracho trees has been the primary source of tannery tannin. (Current tanning practices primarily use inorganic tanning agents.) They are equally significant in both gymnosperms and angiosperms. Gymnosperms are plants that have seeds unprotected by an ovary or fruit. They include conifers such as sequoias, cycads, and ginkgo. Angiosperms are plants with flowers and produce seeds enclosed within a carpel. A very large group, they include herbaceous plants, shrubs, grasses, and most trees.

Tannins are critical ingredients in the longevity of sequoias. Infused throughout the bark, they protect these titans from bacteria and fungi by precipitating out enzymes and other protein exudates. This action prevents potentially destructive organisms from infecting, and ultimately sickening, the trees. Thanks primarily to tannins, sequoias enjoy continued and sustained growth throughout their lifetimes.

But sequoias also have another preservative trait. Botanically speaking, bark is an accumulation of various outer layers of a wood plant. It consists of tissues outside the vascular cambium, or central bundle of vascular cells. As long as they are alive, sequoias annually increase the thickness of their bark, an expanse up to two feet (0.6 m). This ever-growing exterior provides sequoias with a natural insulation against ground fire damage. Thick barks infused with tannins are a primary reason for their longevity. And throughout those long lives, they continually grow ever more commanding and ever looming.

Sequoia bark is unusually fire-resilient but not totally incombustible, a factor that clearly differentiates it from other conifers. Equally important is that the high levels of tannin in sequoia wood makes the trees practically immune to fungal diseases or insects. Nevertheless, both will attack (but not destroy) the tree. The sequoia bark beetle (*Phloeosinus rubicundulus*), a frequent visitor, often creates short longitudinal galleries beneath the bark, most notably on felled or dying sequoias.

As with most ancient trees, sequoia longevity is measured in rings. The oldest authenticated specimen is the Muir Snag at approximately 3,500 years old. Although it is dead, it is about 140 feet (42.6 m) tall and still stands in the Converse Basin of Giant Sequoia National Monument. Next in line is a stump, known as CBR26, in Giant Sequoia National Monument that tops out at 3,266 years. Third in line is another stump (D-21), a 3,220-year-old remnant in the Sequoia National Forest. Then there is the President Tree, a living titan standing along Congress Trail in Sequoia National Park. This specimen, at 3,200 years old, is the third largest sequoia in the world and the oldest-known living sequoia on the planet. Its germination coincided with the solar eclipse of April 16, 1178 BCE, the termination of the Late Bronze Age, the end of the Hittite Empire along with the cultural collapse of the Mycenaean kingdoms, and the Battle of the Delta when the Egyptian pharaoh Ramesses III turned back a major sea invasion.

Sequoia National Park is an environment of superlatives: an ecosystem of lazuline lakes, sweeping meadows, ascending mountains, and of course, groves of resplendent trees that cast their millennia-old shadows across a splendid landscape.

On one visit in late May we set out from the town of Three Rivers. Indigo skies wrapped around the gray-tipped mountains of the Sierra Nevada. Myriad streams coursed through deep ravines and broad golden valleys. The foothills full of chaparral, oak and riparian woodlands, and mixed-conifer forests frequently offered an array of spring wildflowers sprinkled amongst rich geological formations. This was an ageless canvas of nature's finest hues splashed across a vast tectonic landscape awaiting our discovery. (One writer describes Sequoia National Park as "the Michelangelo of the Natural World.") A brief stop at Ash Mountain entrance and a one-mile (1.6 km) climb up General's Highway brought us to the Foothills Visitor Center and park headquarters.

After perusing the displays, we continued our journey up the mountain and parked at the main Sherman Tree trailhead. Hiking sticks in hand, we joined throngs of visitors for the short walk downhill that brought us to the largest and most famous of giant sequoias, named General Sherman. In mid-September 2021, the KNP Complex fire, a lightning-caused wildfire, burned upslope toward the Giant Forest and General Sherman. Firefighters worked feverishly to wrap protective foil around the lower ten to fifteen feet (3–4.5 m) of the tree. The material minimized the likelihood fire would ignite exposed areas such as old fire scars. The tree survived, but barely.

The tree is gigantic, nearly incomprehensibly so. The estimated weight of the trunk is 1,385 tons, equivalent to the weight of 213 African elephants. Its overall height is 274.9 feet (83.7 m), the length of three-quarters of a football field. Its circumference at ground level is 102.6 feet (31 m), the length of a Boeing 737-500 jet aircraft. Its maximum diameter is 36.5 feet (11.1 m), the width of a tennis court. Its average crown spread is 106.5 feet (32.5 m), two-thirds the length of an Olympic swimming pool. The volume of its trunk measures 52,500 cubic feet, more than half the volume of that pool. By volume, it is the largest-known living, single-stem tree on Earth. Also noteworthy is the fact that a sequoia's roots can spread out over more than an acre (0.4 ha), an embrace of over 90,000 cubic feet (2,549 m³) of soil. That mass of matted roots has to maintain the equilibrium of a tree that weighs two million pounds (907,000 kg).

Sprouting at about the same time as Julius Caesar was born, General Sherman's estimated age is between 2,100 and 2,200 years old. This estimate was determined in 2000 by Nate Stephenson of the US Geological Survey's Sierra Nevada Global Change Research Program. Stephenson used a mathematical formula to calculate the ages of giant trees based on his study of the rings in the sawn stumps of old sequoias.

Before the advent of current dendrochronological precision, scientists assumed the tree to be nearly 6,000 years old, with some estimates even extending the tree's longevity to an unbelievable 11,000 years. In the 1960s, they adjusted the age to 3,500 years, then later recalculated it to 2,500 years, and now it stands at its current numbers. The ideal conditions that surround it have enabled its rapid growth, making it taller than other older sequoias. General Sherman, like all mature sequoias, will continue to grow throughout its lifetime. Each year it adds enough wood to make another sixty-foot (18 m)-tall tree.

After a half hour of observation, photography, and note-taking, I depart from the crowd surrounding General Sherman and head east for the tranquility and calm of Congress Trail. I arc down along the paved trail, cross Sherman Creek on a wooden bridge, and traverse a hillside sprinkled with giant sequoias. The trail patiently climbs up and over a low ridge and past an impressive group of trees in the heart of the forest. From there, the trail makes a right and then a left to loop past the Senate, House, and Founders groups, a concentration of distinctive mammoths including the aforementioned President Tree, the Chief Sequoyah Tree, the General Lee Tree, the Lincoln Tree, and the McKinley Tree.

Sequoias, I suspect, have a way of tapping into our consciousness and making us more aware of our surroundings. As with all of nature, they improve us. Richard Louv, in his compelling and inspirational book *Last Child in the Woods: Saving Our Children From Nature-Deficit Disorder*, notes, "A growing body of research links our mental, physical, and spiritual health directly to our association with nature—in positive ways. Several of these studies suggest that thoughtful exposure . . . to nature can even be a powerful form of therapy." Beneath the canopies, I felt an awareness of simple things, and peaceful thoughts enveloped my mind. So too, was I reminded of naturalist E. O. Wilson's prophetic words, "Because we evolved in nature, we have a biological need to connect with it."

Equally significant was the inescapable conclusion that my walks through and around sequoias were an entrance into a kind of religion. There is an indomitable spirit here. As the forester and writer Peter Wohlleben observes, a forest of trees exudes something akin to pheromones—a sensory stimulant that alerts other trees that there might be danger close by, an approaching forest fire or a swarm of leaf-eating insects bent on reducing foliage. Saunter into this realm of giant trees, and "something akin to pheromones" will envelope you, encase you, and wrap you in their embrace, not only for the time you are there but for long days after.

The sermon is ever-present. However, no booming voice, no "shoulds" or "should nots," it floats on the air like the wisp of butterfly wings or the scratch of a grub locked beneath thick bark. This is nature's lesson: a persistent cant of long-standing wisdom encased in seeds, embraced by giants, and germinated by time. The admonitions are forever shared on small eddies, wrapped among leafy branches, and infused into the tangle of deep-soil roots gripping the earth.

William Tweed, now retired, was for twenty-eight years the chief naturalist for Sequoia National Park. His book *King Sequoia: The*

Tree That Inspired a Nation, Created our National Park System, and Changed the Way We Think about Nature shares a passionate discourse about sequoias and the signature park in which they live. I tracked him down to his home in Oregon, and we arranged for a Zoom interview to talk about his extensive knowledge of sequoias.

I was curious as to why humans need to understand the longevity of trees. Tweed told me that most people miss the point that longevity is an evolutionary trait, simply one of a large number of different possible strategies that an organism can use to survive. The logic is that the organisms that exist today on our planet are the ones that have found a way to survive. If they don't find a way to survive, they're not here and their genes disappear. Longevity is built into the genes of certain organisms. He went on to point out that when we look at the world of plants, we have successful organisms like bristlecone pines and sequoias that live for multiple millennia and tiny annual wildflowers that live for only a few weeks. And it's not that one strategy is more successful than the other, because they both survive. And so, as Tweed put it, both are successful, it's just that they're using profoundly different strategies.

He made the point that there are many more organisms that survive with short life spans in large numbers than organisms that survive with long life spans and by implication, relatively fewer numbers. Ultimately, in a successful forest, all an individual sequoia needs to do is replace itself, and it has a couple of thousands of years to do that.

This spawned another query on how sequoias stand apart from other old trees. Tweed answered that in most ways, they do not. They are just big green plants. However, he was careful to offer a few exceptions, the most distinctive one being that sequoias combine two attributes that are not common. First, they're long-lived. Second, they do something that is rare even among long-living organisms: they are very fast growing. As he stated, trees, like sequoias, grow as long as they live. Consequently, if sequoias live a long time, they grow fast, and grow as long as they live, they will end up being really big.

Tweed was careful to point out that trees have practical, physical limits to their height. The taller a tree gets, the more difficult it is to move moisture and nutrients up the trunk. Even in good environments there are limits. The tallest trees on Earth come relatively close to matching each other in maximum height. That may not be a coincidence. That may be telling us something about physical limits of moving moisture. Many types of trees top out between two hundred and three hundred feet (61–91 m) tall, and only a few exceed that. The tallest of the California redwoods reach heights of 360 to 370 feet (109–111 m). But, at the same time, trees continue to get thicker and thicker as long as they live, and sequoias do that really well. That, he said, really accounts for their excessive bulk, which is how they get to be the world's largest trees by volume, if not by height.

Tweed went on to observe that the big challenge for sequoias is, unsurprisingly, fire. Sequoias grow in a world that has a dry season and a wet season, a Mediterranean climate. In general, there are relatively wet winters and long, dry summers. The summers have occasional thunderstorms, and as a result the Sierra Nevada has always had summer lightning-sparked fires. He emphasized that sequoias are designed to survive these fires. Scientists, studying rings and scars, can actually date past fires in sequoias through the study of tree rings on living and dead trees. As a result, he noted, we have a fire chronology for sequoia groves that goes back at least five thousand to six thousand years. During all that time the groves burned regularly and therefore not very intensely.

When trees burn frequently, they don't accumulate an enormous amount of fuel, and the sequoias are well designed to handle that. They have a thick, highly fire-resistant bark, and the bark burns very slowly, if at all, and keeps out heat. The sequoias are thus equipped to live with periodic fire. A sequoia that has lived for several thousand years has likely survived an enormous number of fires. Tweed recalled that visitors often look at a tree and ask, "When was the fire that scarred the tree?" His usual answer was, "That wasn't the result of a single fire, that's the composite result of dozens and dozens of fires." His response often changes the perspective from "When did the tree get hurt?" to "Look how tough the tree has been."

I wanted to know what he considered the greatest threat to the longevity of sequoias. He explained that sequoias grow on the lower edge of the snowbelt between five thousand and seven thousand feet (1,524–2,134 m). But because of climate change, the temperature of the Sierras is rising. Over the last several years, it's gone up by about one degree Celsius (1.8° F). When it has increased by two degrees Celsius (3.6° F), according to Tweed, then all the old, established sequoias will be growing in the wrong environment. This will be a significant crisis for the trees.

He also pointed to the current drought, which as of this writing has lasted for twenty years. When something goes on for twenty years, it's not a temporary feature—it has an air of permanence. This prolonged dryness is making the world of the sequoias more inhospitable for them. Not only are the temperatures rising and insects moving into new environments, but the fire season is also getting longer and the amount of moisture in the soil is dropping. All these things, Tweed emphasized, are fundamental threats to organisms like sequoias that have been living in a very narrow niche for a long time.

As we were talking in the summer of 2022, Tweed observed that in the previous three years there had been massive damage to old-growth sequoias that had never occurred before in the 150 years humans have tried to protect and manage them. He noted that a lot of supposedly fire-resistant sequoias found themselves in fires so hot and intense that they simply were not resistant enough. As a result, once-vibrant groves now may simply be gone biologically. All the sequoias in those places died, something that has never happened in our experience or in the tree-ring record. He added, "All of that speaks directly to the future of sequoias and their longevity. The implication is, I think, we're going to have to work a lot harder to protect and perpetuate the groves we still have because it's not easy to replace an old-growth sequoia grove."

Tweed's words reminded me that humans have a decided and continuous impact on the longevity of trees, particularly magnificent ones such as sequoias. Too often, however, good intentions are superseded by display and arrogance. Take, for example, the General Noble Tree, an impressive sequoia which by the late nineteenth century had reached an astounding height of 312 feet (95.1 m) and an equally astounding age of 3,200 years. In 1892, someone decided to fell the tree to create a natural history exhibit for the forthcoming 1893 World's Columbian Exposition in Chicago. As a result, the tree was subsequently toppled and divided into forty-six sections, loaded onto eleven railroad cars, and shipped to Chicago, where it was "reassembled" and put on display. There, it was unfortunately tagged with the moniker "California Hoax," since many attendees did not believe that a tree that size was real. Today, its remains, known as the Chicago Stump, can be visited along the Chicago Stump Trail in the Converse Basin Grove of Sequoia National Park. It is a 0.6 mile (.97 m) round-trip hike to and from the often unbelievable hubris of humankind.

As humans, we have both influence and impact on the planet. As the putatively most intelligent beings on this sphere, we are charged with using that force of mind to preserve the world we inhabit. Global warming, for example, isn't just happening on its own. It is the result of actions endorsed and promulgated by supposedly well-knowing humans. The decisions we have made in the past and the laws we pass today have a moral and profound effect on the world our children and grandchildren inherit tomorrow. Indeed, Walt Kelly's comic strip *Pogo*, in 1970, coined a phrase that still resonates today, particularly in discussions of sequoias: "We have met the enemy and he is us."

Late one afternoon, with wisps of clouds overhead, we took intermission on a park bench. The sun had begun to settle in the western sky, families of tired children and exhausted parents had bundled their belongings and began the trek toward the nearest shuttle bus, and the two of us absorbed the deepening silence. The midday cacophony had diminished, and we were at one with the tenor of the forest. Our quiet conversation was one of admiration and respect for a species that dwarfed us in both size and time.

Within a long moment of observation, I watched a longhorn beetle (*Phymatodes nitidus*) scramble its way across the surface of a fallen colossus, the size differential beyond words. A sudden glint of sunlight embraced the creature, momentarily held it, then released it as it sauntered to the other side of the fallen giant. It was a slice of time, part of a flow that human interlopers usually do not see. It was also an extension of the life of the forest, a signature repeated over the millennia in testament to the continuum of life in this ancient place.

I paused to observe the singular skeleton of a once magnificent sequoia, felled by fire. But this time I saw something new. Scattered about the remains of its carbonized trunk were about a dozen tiny saplings, each about a foot (0.3 m) tall and sprouting an array of evergreen branches whose vibrant color contrasted with the blackness of the earth. These miniature parishioners, genus *Sequoiadendron*, stood in solemn silence before a once-grand tree. I was in awe of these saplings' natural determination to repopulate and bring this ground back to life, slow evolutionary step by slow evolutionary step.

A new generation of sequoia seedlings surround a parent tree
in Sequoia National Park.

The seedlings were a biological reminder that nature knows
how to take care of its own. Seeds are deposited in soil, plants
germinate and sprout, trees grow, and a forest becomes a living
and active community, a place where many grow while others
succumb to factors and fires. A forest is an organism, one that lives
and dies, reproduces and recycles. So, too, does it expand and
contract: expanding via water, nutrients, and geographical positioning, contracting via insects, diseases, rot, and, of course, the
inevitable fire.

As humans, we frequently, though not always, admire that
cycle. We embrace the determined longevity and prodigious
heights of these stately trees. We applaud the dimensions of their
lives—particularly when those dimensions exceed expectations.
We celebrate their out-of-the-ordinary existence. We cheer
their lives.

We stand, heads craned upward, in admiration.

Part III

Standing
Alone

Several distinguished trees have stood firmly rooted against an array of environmental threats. They are supreme against the elements and mighty in the face of nature's challenges. They are elegant individuals of strength and determination. They are resolute against the odds.

Here are individuals that have weathered a plethora of life-threatening events. For long years they have stood staunchly against natural forces determined to topple them over or shorten their lives. Responding to genetic imperatives, each did what it needed to do to maintain its "tree-ness." Throughout their lives, these trees bent, shook, and swayed, but, at least metaphorically speaking, they never lost sight of a future existence.

Here you will discover a sylvan beauty within sight of the Mississippi River, one that has outlasted the cataclysmic power of cyclical hurricanes and come away relatively unscathed. You will make the acquaintance of a scrubby and seemingly undistinguished plant that, in a distant life, had giant sloths and grazing mastodons as neighbors. And you will travel a hard road to view a singular individual that persists in spite of fiery threats and biologic interference.

Persistence is ingrained in the makeup of these striking trees. Their grit and fortitude will entrance you. Their mettle, as you will discover, is a constant, one reflected in both stature and age. Most important, these are silent sentinels of time, masterful environmental pillars, and firm beacons of botanical endurance. They are resilient. Equally important, they are ancient.

Prehistoric Roots

Common name: Palmer's Oak, Jurupa Oak,
Hurunga Oak
Scientific binomial: *Quercus palmeri*
Age: ~13,000 years
Location: Riverside County,
southern California

10,979 BCE, Tierra del Fuego, Chile
The summer sun rested on the horizon, a blood-red orb that
covered the land with light but brought scant warmth to the
Indigenous peoples who roamed across the extensive frontier and
who called this seemingly barren landscape home. Even clear days
spawned bitterly cold winds that eddied and swirled into the caves
and rock shelters built against the palisades of tall mountains. The
blisteringly frigid winds whipped across bare rocks and scattered
stones, often without relief. Constant storms indiscriminately tore
plants from their roots and stunted the growth of the meager trees
hugging the coast. Rain was ever-present, everything from drizzles
to squalls pelted the hills and ran into a network of streams and
rivers. The cycles of weather were both constant and brusque. This
was a terrain of climatological extremes and a life of
unceasing hardships.

The people of this brutal landscape were the Yaghans,
members of five related groups that have inhabited the Tierra del
Fuego archipelago for thousands of years. Ancient Yaghans

customarily wore little if any clothing. To protect themselves from the elements they covered their bodies with a thick layer of animal fat. They huddled around constant fires, and they rested by squatting close to the ground to reduce their surface area and conserve heat. Often regarded as the southernmost peoples in the world, they still live in this harsh and violent land, although today their numbers have dwindled to less than two thousand.

Fourteen-year-old Wanakipa stood on the rocky shore with three other girls. Like her friends, she wore a single garment of animal skin wrapped loosely across her shoulders. Nearby was a small fire tended by her cousin. The girls were intent on watching their mothers dive into the surf, submerge themselves in the bitterly cold water, and capture shellfish for a communal dinner.

Their clan consisted of thirty-eight individuals—a collection of five families with children ranging from newborns to teenagers. Wanakipa's family consisted of her parents, two sisters, and one brother. As the oldest, she often assumed many chores such as babysitting, cooking and gathering firewood. Quite often, she would need to walk great distances to locate fallen branches of nires and lenga trees, deciduous species native to southern Chile and Argentina. Forests of these trees were often distributed over rugged mountain slopes from sea level to elevations of two thousand feet (600 m).

Wanakipa's father was a hunter. Often he and the other men in the clan would go out in their canoes for many days searching for sea lions. When they found one, the men would surround it, throw their spears, and pelt it with stones until it succumbed to the onslaught. They would then strip its skin and carefully divide the meat into several portions for transport back to the clan to be cooked over small charcoal ovens. They saved the animal fat, that essential commodity to ward off the cold.

It was not unusual for the nomadic clan to frequently collect their meager belongings and move a few miles up or down the coast in their continuous search for food and the geological overhangs and caves necessary for shelter. Migrations were a consistent way of life, a reality to sustain themselves in this ruthless land. It was a constant of life in a most frigid clime.

10,979 BCE, Southern California

In the low hills 7,122 miles (11,461 km) north of Tierra del Fuego, a forbidding creature lumbered over a rolling plain. It spent its days dragging its ponderous body—ten feet (3.1 m) long, over 2,200 pounds (998 kg) in weight—across the muddy prehistoric landscape in search of vegetation to satiate its robust appetite. It was one of three genera of ground sloths—*Nothrotheriops*, *Megalonyx*, and *Paramylodon*—huge fauna that lived in what is now southern California from the Middle Pleistocene epoch (~150,000 years ago) to the Late Pleistocene epoch (~11,700 years ago).

Megalonyx ranged far outside California: the creature's species, *Megalonyx jeffersonii*, was named in honor of President Thomas Jefferson, who obtained and described several fossil bones from West Virginia in 1797. Unlike its contemporaries, *M. jeffersonii* was the only ground sloth to range as far north as present-day Alaska.

Like other species of ground sloths, it had a blunt snout, massive jaw, and large peglike teeth. Its rear legs ended in flat feet that allowed it to rear up into select Pleistocene trees to feed on succulent leaves. Unlike most ground mammals, the heelbone and the outside edge of the foot bore the weight of the giant sloth. As a result, it walked with a waddling motion. *Megalonyx* means "giant claw," and it was able to use its extended appendages to rake leaves from willow branches, its favorite food, and shrubs in this mixed conifer-hardwood habitat. The other species of ground sloths in the area survived on different food sources such as yucca, Joshua trees, and cacti, which may have eliminated intraspecies competition for the same resources.

The giant sloth was one of many creatures, including mastodons, smilodons, short-faced bears, and several species of tapirs, that inhabited this domain. Also included was the enormous *Glyptotherium*, a massive beast up to six feet (1.8 m) long and one ton (907 kg) in weight. This was a creature physiologically similar to modern-day armadillos, one with an enormous frame covered by a body armor of bony deposits called osteoderms.

For long centuries, conditions in this geography were favorable for many animals. But eventually the distinctive megafauna of this era died out during what is known as the Pleistocene extinction (~13,000–11,700 years ago). Some paleontologists speculate that climate change was to blame. Specifically, the formation and eventually shifting of ice sheets across the North American continent significantly altered the growth, availability, and distribution of food sources, particularly for large herbivores. Scientists conjecture that the ability of megafauna to browse and forage significantly decreased over time as they attempted to adjust to a constantly changing environment.

Other scientists embrace the Pleistocene overkill hypothesis, a theory underscoring the existence of archeological evidence suggesting that the arrival of the first humans in the Americas and the first megafauna extinctions occurred almost in historical concert with each other. A few experts hypothesize that a pandemic disease of some sort may have ultimately leveled all these unique critters, including the giant sloths and Glyptotheriums.

But one plant, against all environmental and ecological odds, survived.

Present Day

I spent the earliest years of my childhood climbing trees, biking suburban neighborhoods, and diligently attending school in West Los Angeles, California. On special times of the year, our family would travel to the Wilshire District of Los Angeles proper, a grand assembly of dignified homes surrounded by tall hedges, well-manicured lawns, and long rows of deciduous trees, to visit my grandparents, typically on Thanksgiving and Christmas. While there, my two sisters and I would ask our grandfather if we could see his cherished medical instruments, stored in a small bedroom in back of the kitchen pantry. My grandfather, Dr. Wirt B. Dakin, was a urologist in private practice in Los Angeles for sixty-three years. He was also the long-standing historian for the American Urological Association. He was born on November 23, 1883, and passed away on May 15, 1975. That is, he lived for ninety-one years, five months, and eight days at a time when life expectancy for males born in the United States in 1883 was just slightly more than forty-two years. I especially admired him for that.

A little more than fifty miles (80 km) east of my grandfather's former office lives an organism whose continuing age is 12,909 years more than my grandfather's life. That is, it has lived for 143 of my grandfather's lifetimes.

It is a Palmer oak, *Quercus palmeri*. An inconspicuous and seemingly inconsequential plant, this specimen grows on a stony hillside just beyond the perimeter of Riverside, California. It is a dignified and ancient tree—one whose life span encompasses the domestication of sheep (~11,000 BCE), the cultivation of wheat (~8,000 BCE), Hammurabi's Code of Law (1755–1750 BCE), the end of the Tang dynasty (907 CE), the birth of William Shakespeare (1564 CE), two twentieth-century world wars, and the election of Barack Obama (2008 CE).

Unlike towering forest denizens such as the Douglas fir, Coulter pine, and knobcone pine of the nearby Santa Ana Mountains, *Quercus palmeri* are most often medium to large, 6 to 9.8 feet (2–3 m) xerophytic evergreen shrubs with multiple trunks and sharp holly-like leaves, stiff with waxy edges. Members of the beech family (*Fagaceae*), these slow-growing organisms typically have a compact

A leaf cluster, with acorns, is part of the long-lived Palmer's Oak near Riverside, California.

and shrubby appearance, with most of its reddish-brown twigs branched at 65–90° angles and others angling down to the ground.

Trunks can be up to eight inches (20.3 cm) in diameter, with medium-gray bark that is moderately furrowed and often flakey. Like most oaks, the Palmer is monoecious, sporting both male and female flowers. Pollination takes place in the spring, with the acorns ripening approximately eighteen months later. Both the acorns and leaves contain abundant tannic acid, its acrid taste warding off infestation by nibbling insects. So, too, do the tannins deter the encroachment of several fungal diseases. According to Brian Powell, who has studied the flora of southern California extensively, *Quercus palmeri* sometimes hybridizes with other species of oak within overlapping ranges.

This specific Palmer oak is an indistinct ground-hugging clonal organism, one frequently missed or ignored by casual passersby. Also known as the Jurupa Oak, since it lives in the Jurupa Hills of Riverside County, it occupies a short gulch between two large granite boulders situated on a rocky and north-facing slope at an elevation of 1,200 feet (366 m). The specimen has approximately seventy stem clusters forming a dense thicket about three feet (0.9 m) in height and extending over an area of roughly eighty-two by twenty-six feet (198 sq m). Researchers speculate that its normal height has declined over the millennia through a combination of expansive droughts, frequent fires, and powerful winds. Andrew Sanders, who has studied the tree extensively, relates that this specimen has survived massive biotic changes over many thousands of years and appears to be a last living remnant of a vanished woody vegetative regime that occupied the inland valleys of what is now southern California at the height of the last ice age. According to Sanders, the Jurupa Oak is most likely a relic of an ecosystem that no longer exists, having found a foothold on this undistinguished escarpment at a time when enormous bison and ancient camels roamed the area.

Normally this type of oak occupies higher elevations, 2,953 feet (900 m) to 4,921 feet (1,500 m) above sea level, inhabiting canyons, mountain washes, and chapparal thickets primarily in mesic habitats—that is, temperate and reasonably well-watered zones next to drier country—and desert outposts from northern Baja California, Mexico, to just north of San Francisco, California. However, during a cooler and wetter time, this particular specimen took root and flourished in its present low-altitude location. Then, near the end of the Pleistocene era, the climate changed abruptly, becoming hotter and drier, resulting in a die-out of the plant's contemporaries. It was now one of a kind. As Jeffrey Ross-Ibarra, of the University of California, Davis, has stated, the Jurupa Oak scrapes by in dry chaparral, wedged between granite boulders and stunted by high winds, atop a small hill in plain sight of suburban backyards. Like the Joshua tree, it is a relic of another time; a survivor of the ages.

As I began my own investigations into the life of this Palmer's oak, I surrounded myself with photos of the old-timer retrieved from select scientific journals, regional Southern California publications, and an array of amateur photos tucked away in distant corners of the internet. I was looking for a magnificent oak, yet I saw only a low-branching, undistinguished, shrubby plant. It crouched on a short incline in the manner of the hum-drum ground cover mechanically planted inside the median strips of California highways to give substance to otherwise bare soil. What I saw was certainly not magnificent or eye-catching, but simply an undistinguished plant clinging to a precarious life.

According to a groundbreaking research study published in the online journal *PLoS ONE* on December 23, 2009, a team of scientists based primarily at University of California, Davis, began the process of dating the Jurupa Oak. In the article they discussed how they initially collected leaf tissue from across the site, including from thirty-two of the seventy stem clusters. An analysis of the proteins from those samples demonstrated low genetic variation, implying a clonal organism. In short, all the samples were clones of each other.

During onsite excavations the researchers noted insufficient amounts of ancient wood in or around the plant. They speculated that this absence was the result of extensive and persistent termite activity over the years. Consequently, it was impossible to date any found wood via radiocarbon dating. According to their report, the scientists decided to count the annual growth rings in multiple stem cross-sections. This would allow them to determine an average growth rate for the clone as a whole. To do that, they collected transverse sections of ten dead stems and one live branch from different locations within the site. They then air-dried, finely sanded, and in some cases stained the cross-sections to make annual growth rings visible. The scientists estimated ring counts and diameters manually from digital images of the sections.

The research team was able to determine the age of the Palmer oak clone through a direct observation of the number of annual growth rings present over a given distance in individual cross-section of the samples. For verification, they also measured growth rates in two populations of Palmer oaks at other southern California locations. This allowed team members to compare the average growth of Palmer oaks under varying environmental conditions.

The resulting observations revealed a growth rate of 0.03 ± 0.0008 inches (0.8 ± 0.02 mm) per year, which, when compared to the overall size of the plant (2,132 sq. ft. or 200 sq. m), resulted in an estimated age range of approximately $15,600 \pm 2,500$ years. The authors noted that this was their most credible approximation of the age of the clone, since it takes into account a wide range of growth conditions. Additionally, they stated that their most realistic estimate, based on stems collected from a variety of environmental conditions, is that the clone is at least 13,000 years old. As such, it rivals two other ancient bushes (not trees), a creosote bush in the Mojave Desert of California (~11,700 years old) and a solitary box huckleberry in south-central Pennsylvania (~13,000 years old). Writing in *National Geographic*, science journalist Ed Yong noted that the scientists were working from conservative assumptions and that the tree is very likely older still.

The researchers concluded their article with both a warning and a speculation. First, they suggested that global warming, since the end of the last ice age, may have pushed the ideal elevation of *Quercus palmeri* higher into the surrounding mountains. As a result, this singular tree, a remnant of another age, now lives in an isolated and environmentally unprotected territory. Yet the team also surmises that cloning may have been a major and significant contributor to the ultimate persistence of this particular plant over time. They conclude their article by stating that "it is tempting to speculate that disjunct populations of many . . . other species may consist of extremely long-lived clones as well."

I find it impressive that natural selection, in Charles Darwin's phrase, has woven its evolutionary tapestry through this ancient expanse of southern California real estate. It is a constant action, influencing organisms of long ago as much as the newly seeded lawns of suburban Riverside County. Its universal maxim is that only the fittest survive while all others succumb to a panoply of genetic imperfections, vagaries of unpleasant climatological shifts across the planet, or repositioning of continents on their ceaseless march from epoch to epoch. It is a botanical truth, and in the case of this Palmer's oak a botanical reality.

This *Quercus palmeri* is a survivor, a remnant of a titanic ice age that has redefined the limits of botanical longevity. An individual in isolation, this tree has endured odds and predictability. I am certain that botanists have yet to discover other specific and select traits that have worked in its evolutionary favor. This plant has demonstrated a unique resilience that warrants our rapt attention and deep admiration. I know of few other plants more charged with their own well-being than this. It is both relic and monument, remarkable as an evolutionary product of a faraway time.

Unsurprisingly for southern California, the area around the oak is experiencing rapid growth and constant development. Commercial ventures, widening highways, shopping malls, spreading tracts of new homes, and the necessary infrastructure for these developments are invading this archaic place. This onslaught severely impacts both the ecology as well as the ultimate survival of the tree. So, too, does it affect tradition and reverence.

Sometimes referred to as the Hurunga Oak by the Gabrieleño Band of Mission Indians/Kizh Nation, the tree bears the name of a settlement that once stood nearby. The Gabrieleño people consider it sacred and revered, a medicine tree like many other oaks, each suffused with special spiritual powers. This specimen is a unique and surviving remnant of Kizh Nation culture and history. The tribe would like to see it preserved and guarded for future generations as both icon and emblem.

Consider that this tree may have persisted in this location in spite of all the encroachments and perils that have challenged it over the centuries. Perhaps its simple purpose may have been to survive for another year or another millennium. We might consider that sense of purpose to be ingrained in its genetic code, and even if bringing teleology into biology is shot through with problems, it is important to remember that living species have hereditary factors beyond their or our control.

We humans have some degree of choice in determining what we will embrace and what we will eschew. In short, we have decision-making power in selecting elements that might extend our personal longevity. Waking up each morning with a clear purpose—writing a book about ancient trees, for example—might be both incentive and stimulant for a long-lived life. Perhaps *Quercus palmeri* shares a similar destiny.

Rachel Sussman, who has made a photographic study of the Jurupa Oak, underscores the resiliency of this ancient specimen when she notes that it has quietly persisted on public land even as housing developments, a cement factory, containers filled with modular home components, and the traffic of off-road vehicles become its new neighbors. In its early years, this tree contended with herbivorous megafauna. Today, 130 centuries later, its enemies are an encroachment of subdivisions, the escalation of climate change, the rubbish of civilization, and the invasion of devil-may-care bikers whose single-track trails slice ever closer to it. And while this Palmer's oak has successfully endured countless environmental stressors and catastrophes, it is unlikely to withstand the blades of bulldozers.

Nevertheless, it survives. For now.

CHAPTER 9

Sequestered Icon

Common name: Sierra Western Juniper, Sierra
Juniper, Western Juniper, Bennett Juniper
Scientific Binomial: *Juniperus grandis*
Age: 3,000± years
Location: Stanislaus National Forest,
Tuolumne County, California

~1578 BCE, Çeşme-Bağlararası, Western Turkey

The summer was piercing. Windows and doors stood open,
allowing offshore winds to blow through and temper the prevailing
heat. Garments were light and open for both high-ranking politi-
cians as well as the many laborers who worked in and around this
coastal city. The colors of clothing, buildings, and furniture often
ranged from whites to beiges—a nod to the cooling effects, both
physical and psychological, of light hues.

Two months previously, Enayat turned ten and enjoyed a
grand celebration with his parents and five sisters. He was a
gregarious and pleasant lad liked by almost everyone in the town.
He often helped elderly people carry heavy baskets or tend their
gardens, often on his own initiative and never for pay. When not
in school or working in his father's shop, Enayat roamed the city
streets or journeyed to the waterfront with his dog and constant
companion. If a townsperson saw one, it was certain that the
other was close at hand. The two of them took meals together,

slept together, and played ball games along the wide, sweeping beach that wrapped around the town. Theirs was an idyllic life full of fun and frolic. Indeed, Enayat's friends often told him that his dog was the older brother he never had. Enayat smiled when he heard that.

One day, the distant Mediterranean island of Thera blew apart in one of the most violent and massive volcanic eruptions in human memory, an eruption that has since been categorized as a level 7 (out of 8) on the volcanic explosivity index. Rock and debris torpedoed across the sea and into the air for miles around. A high-altitude cloud of volcanic ash surged into the atmosphere. The immediate eruption destroyed cities, wiped away vast acres of fertile farmland, and submerged long stretches of coastline. Hours later, the townspeople of Çeşme-Bağlararası, miles away, watched in horror and disbelief as the waters in the bay receded, then began to swell. Water rose up the shore and swept into the village, not in a towering wave but rather as a powerful surge that caught everyone by surprise. No one could believe what they were seeing.

It was an oceanic monster—a tsunami.

Once again, the ocean receded and rose up. As before, a wall of water washed over the landscape, through the streets, and into the fields beyond. Entire groves of olive trees, the life and sustenance of the village, were ripped to shreds and swept away by the power of the tsunami. Their shallow roots, although embedded in the earth for long years, could not resist the great oceanic force.

The second wave retreated, and then the remaining survivors saw the most terrifying sight—an enormous wall of water as high as the tallest tree. The water crashed through homes, crushed buildings, and swallowed townspeople. Boards, branches, and debris scattered everywhere. Hundreds of people were swept out to sea. It was one of the most cataclysmic and disastrous tsunamis in recorded history. The destruction was enormous, the loss of life unfathomable.

~1578 BCE, Tuolomne County, California
More than one hundred million years ago, great masses of granite
formed deep underground in the region of the North American
continent now known as eastern California. Less than five million
years ago, the range started to uplift and glacial erosion exposed
the granite, creating the mountains and cliffs of the Sierra Nevada.
The oldest rocks, both metamorphic and sedimentary, formed a
wide range of elevations characteristic of this region. Over the
millennia, retreating ice age glaciers stripped the landscape of
sustainable soils. The terrain was mostly volcanic bedrock. This
was hardly an environment for viable plant life or migratory animals. Yet that bedrock, over tens of thousands of years, eventually
became a carpet of soil that nourished low-growing sagebrush,
a few junipers, and scattered stands of lodgepole pines.

Predictable conditions marked the period after the last ice
age, the Middle Archaic period, from 2000 BCE to 500 CE: winters
were harsh and unforgiving, but warm summers yielded robust
fields of grass. Both the climate and the environment sustained
life in many forms. Water sources were abundant: lakes were
plentiful, and rivers and streams coursed down from the mountains and across spreading valleys.

Human congregations in the area were loose-knit, typically
a few families who shared chores and responsibilities. The tribes
were mainly hunters and gatherers. Their nomadic lifestyle
allowed them to stalk a wide variety of wildlife as well as forage for
roots, seeds, and other sustaining plant life. They produced a wide
range of tools including pestles and mortars, and hunting imple-
ments such as atlatls and spears, crafted from basalt or obsidian.

Around three thousand years ago, an insignificant juniper
seed, similar in size to a popcorn kernel, fell on a dry patch of soil
some 6,875 miles (11,065 km) to the far west of Çeşme-Bağlararası.
In these metamorphic mountains it took only a small amount of
moisture for the seed to germinate and sink its tiny roots into the

substrate. The tree prospered, undisturbed by humans and resilient to the extremes of its landing. In later years, it would gain neighbors who also succeeded and provided company. But it was the elder tree that defied expectations by surviving, quite possibly, more than thirty centuries of winter blizzards and penetrating summer heat. It was a determined and persistent beacon of sustainability and survival.

Present Day

Imagine living in an environment with months of freezing temperatures, constantly howling subzero winds, a soil that is both nutrient-poor and exceedingly thin, a terrain consisting of dry, rocky slopes with shallow intersecting gullies, a water supply both inconsistent and infrequent, deep and expansive winter snows, and a reduced oxygen level of 15.1 percent. You would be living in a temperate coniferous forest, a subalpine ecoregion, and at an elevation of anywhere from 330 feet (100 m) to 10,170 feet (3,100 m) above sea level. Were you a juniper tree, you might find those environmental conditions to be just right for your growth and eventual longevity.

Situated close to Eagle Meadows, a part of the Stanislaus National Forest, the Bennett Juniper is a singular tree that dominates a site heavily glaciated during the previous ice age. Because of that glacial scraping, the soil declined from depths of twenty-four inches (61 cm) to just six inches (15.2 cm). The underlying bedrock is volcanic, with a sagebrush overgrowth along with a random assembly of young lodgepole pines and junipers. Ground-hugging vegetation is sparse and often dry from the drought that has plagued the Sierra since 2000. Those contemporaries, like the Bennett, typically grow on gravely sediment known as glacial till left behind from the retreat of glaciers in the distant past.

The tree's name honors naturalist Clarence Bennett, who studied western juniper trees (*Juniperus occidentalis*) along the

Pacific coast in the early 1890s. His field observations included a collection of fallen branches at various sites, which he used to meticulously count core rings and determine the growth rates of the trees as well as their estimated ages. His measurements indicated that many of those trees were at least one thousand years old.

Basque sheepherders who roamed this area in the 1920s discovered the tree that was to bear his name. Longtime rancher Ed Burgeson introduced it to Bennett in 1932. He guided Bennett to the location and showed him an enormous western juniper more than seventy-five feet (22.8 m) in height. By 1978 the tree, along with a perimeter of three acres (1.2 ha), came under the stewardship of the Nature Conservancy so that it could be formally protected and preserved. That protection brought the tree's existence to the attention of the public, resulting in increased visitation and significant overuse of the property. The Nature Conservancy monitored the property until June 1987, when it conveyed it to the Save the Redwoods League.

Although not a redwood, the tree came under the protection of the League because at the time no other organizations had the resources to protect the tree and the surrounding property from future timber harvests. Ultimately, the League created a small interpretive trail, constructed a bench placed near the tree, and installed some fencing, along with informative panels describing the tree's history and background. In addition, the League paid for an onsite caretaker during the summer months to act as a docent and protect the site from potential vandals.

In November 2022 a more localized organization, the Mother Lode Land Trust (MLLT), headquartered in Jackson, California, took over management of the site. At the time, Ellie Routt, the executive director of MLLT, referred to the Bennett Juniper as an unrivaled specimen of western juniper, a gnarled and knotted tree that had withstood drought, hard winters, and lightning strikes for

thousands of years. She went on to emphasize that MLLTs owner-
ship of this property ensures local oversight and permanent
protection so that everyone can have the chance to see this amazing tree. As part of the transfer between the two organizations, the
Trust also received $40,000 in seed funding to ensure the tree's
long-term stewardship.

Today, the Bennett Juniper reaches an overall height of
eighty-six feet (26.2 m), eight feet longer than a tennis court, with
an average crown spread of fifty-six feet (17.1 m), twenty feet (6.1 m)
longer than a school bus. The diameter at chest height is a little
more than twelve-and-a-half feet (3.8 m), the height of a mature
male African elephant. Its circumference when last measured at the
4.5-foot (1.4 m) mark was 480 inches (12.2 m), so that it would
take eleven adult humans holding hands to completely encircle
the tree. The Bennett is thus the largest juniper of any type listed
in the National Register of Big Trees and the largest known juniper
tree in the United States.

Juniperus grandis is found exclusively in the western United
States. As previously noted, it often goes by many names, including
western juniper, Sierra western juniper, and Sierra juniper. Some
botanists consider it a subspecies of *Juniperus occidentalis*, a tree
also referred to as western juniper. Most often dioecious, meaning
it has female and male reproductive organs in separate individuals, it will occasionally be monoecious, with female and male
reproductive organs in the same individual.

Although *Juniperus grandis*, as a unique species, is restricted
to a narrow geographical band along the eastern flanks of the
Sierra Nevada range, it shares its genus, *Juniperus*, with some five
dozen other species. Those species make the juniper one of the
most widely distributed plants in the world, inhabiting regions as
diverse as Central America, Asia, the Arctic, and tropical Africa.
Also known for a diversity of shapes and sizes, junipers range from
those with muscular branches and soaring up to 131 feet (40 m) to

Juniper "berries" are botanically not true berries but are instead
female seed cones found on several species of juniper trees.

ground-hugging shrubs with long, heavily foliated branches. Some
botanists consider junipers the most common woody plant in
the world.

Junipers, particularly their berries—though technically they
are not "berries," since they originate from the female seed cones
of juniper plants—have been the source of numerous culinary and
medicinal products since Greek and Roman times. These include
use as a flavoring for gin, a bitter spice used in several northern
European recipes, and an additive to some kinds of Finnish beer.
Native American tribes used the berries as a diuretic, a treatment
for diabetes, and for birth control, as well as a source of fragrances
and dyes.

But perhaps the Bennett Juniper's age is its most compelling
feature. Clarence Bennett, using extrapolations of measurements
from nearby juniper trees, including a cross-section from a
downed sample estimated to be eight hundred years old, originally
assessed the tree's age at more than six thousand years. An unverified report, issued in the 1930s, described a coring and subsequent
estimate of three thousand years for the tree's age. In 1989, a

researcher from the University of Arizona Laboratory of Tree-Ring Research cored the tree, confirming that the Bennett Juniper was roughly three thousand years old.

However, the 1989 sampling revealed a mass of rotten wood approximately two feet (0.6 m) beneath the bark, along with a partially hollow space in the interior. With a significant portion of its interior missing, accurately dating the Bennett Juniper would seem especially problematic. Dendroclimatologist Valerie Trouet pointed out that interior rotting of a tree is often dependent on the species as well as its specific location. For example, trees standing in or near a moist environment will quite often have rotted inner cores.

Yet, Trouet added, there are ways of determining the "rot factor" based on the curvature of the tree rings. To do so, scientists estimate how far away those rings are from the pith. But that really works only if they are five to twenty-five years away. As she explained, if those rings are one hundred or two hundred years away from the center, it will be considerably more difficult to see the difference. In other words, scientists will often look for the degree of rotting on the latest ring they can see. If there is a little bit of rotting, they can make a fairly accurate estimate, but more rotting makes the dating process much more challenging.

Trouet further emphasized that trees do not always produce a ring for every year of growth. In arid climates like those in the Southwest, trees conserve their energy and may not form an annual ring across its entire circumference. Because of this, an accurate record of a tree's growth in rings might be incomplete, depending on where in the tree the coring has taken place. Consequently, the core may only provide a specialized snapshot of a tree's life. Other dendrochronological methods such as estimation based on size or growth rates may then be used to determine an approximation of age. To complicate matters, while some trees may miss an annual ring, others will not. In short, not all the trees in a specific area will miss the same annual ring. This is where the process of cross-dating comes in.

In cross-dating, scientists match tree-ring width patterns among several trees and wood fragments from the same area. This allows dendrochronologists to accurately determine the potential absence of rings across one or more living trees or individual stumps. As you may recall from our discussion of bristlecone pines, a comparison of rings from living specimens with those from nonliving and decidedly older specimens such as timbers used in building or furniture construction allows scientists to construct a chronology dating back several centuries.

The year-by-year, ring-by-ring precision of dendrochronology creates a foothold, a mooring, in the study of complex interactions between human history and climate history. That research gives us a window through which we can examine the interior of certain trees as a way of knowing more about their exterior life, the weather they gave endured over time, the dangers survived, and their place in the historical record.

To underscore the age of the Bennett Juniper specifically and the longevity of juniper trees in general, consider another "ancient," the Scofield Juniper, a specimen frequently cited as the longest-lived of all known and accurately dated juniper trees. Located near Sonora Pass, about ten miles from the Bennett Juniper, the Scofield Juniper, long deceased when first discovered, has been accurately cored and cross-sectioned by the Oxford Tree-Ring Laboratory in Baltimore, Maryland. Scientists there determined that the tree's germination occurred in or around 1520 BCE and that it died in approximately 1155 CE. That gives it an overall age of 2,675 years. According to the Rocky Mountain Tree-Ring Research's Old List, a regularly updated database of ancient trees around the world, the Scofield Juniper is the eighth oldest tree ever discovered. Four of those eight trees are sequoias and two are bristlecone pines, putting the Scofield Juniper in very distinguished company. As a species, junipers are the fourth longest-lived trees in the world following bristlecone pines; the alerce trees (*Fitzroya cupressoides*) of southern Chile and Argentina, which have reached documented ages of up to 3,622 years; and, of course, sequoias.

The ride is arduous for humans and their vehicles. A driver needs to keep both hands firmly on the steering wheel and a careful and cautious eye on the path in order to arrive at the Bennett Juniper site without bodily injury, a car accident, or just plain and simple misdirection. A rocky, sinuous track takes its toll not just on a vehicle's carriage but on one's own skeletal structure as well.

The Bennett Juniper is east of the High Sierra town of Sonora. Travel on Highway 108, pass through the tiny town of Strawberry, drive thirteen more miles, and then turn right on 5N01 toward Eagle Meadows. The journey from this point is mostly dirt roads with a few paved sections. The twelve-mile drive is slow and laborious, but the cavalcade of junipers, sagebrush, and lodgepole pines along the way is interesting enough to make the time pass quickly.

The tree is located at an elevation of 8,400 feet (2,560 m), and snowfall and snowmelt limit access for much of the year. The best times to visit are between mid-June to October. If you are planning a visit, I suggest that you contact the Forest Service Summit Ranger Station for road conditions and precautions. A Stanislaus National Forest map at the Summit Ranger Station in Pinecrest is available to aid drivers before beginning their lumpy-bumpy journey. A high-clearance vehicle is strongly recommended, as are well-padded car seats.

Upon arrival, visitors can park in a small lot and walk along the interpretive trail and across a small bridge for about one hundred yards (91.4 m). All around is a sprinkling of younger trees and long patches of scrubby ground. Just slightly uphill from the tree is a wooden bench from which you can admire the magnitude and grandeur of this patient tree, which may grow as little as one inch (2.5 cm) in a human lifetime.

As you observe this botanical wonder, consider the scene in the late summer of 2018. Sparked by an illegal campfire near the Donnell Reservoir, on the middle fork of the Stanislaus River, a major fire broke out and rapidly spread southward through wilderness areas, public lands, and across forest service roads. The fire, which burned for nearly four months, destroyed fifty-four major and eighty-one minor structures, consuming a grand total of 36,450 acres (147.5 km²). The conflagration at one time came to within a half-mile (0.8 km) of the Bennett Juniper. But after intensive ground and air attacks, firefighters stabilized the fire front and saved the tree.

Approximately, twenty-five yards (22.9 m) from the Bennett are two other impressive junipers, affectionately named "Fred" and "Ginger" after the iconic 1930s and 1940s dance duo of Fred Astaire and Ginger Rogers. Look closely and you will see those two partners in a tender embrace, locked in a timeless dance.

There is a solemnity here, a patient blend of sky and land that spreads the horizon and teases the senses. It is pure wilderness, an unadulterated expanse barely touched by humans. While visitors may walk the trail or stand in consideration of a single tree, they are only temporary interlopers. Nature here does not require our intervention to survive. It has done quite well indeed over eras and epochs on its own.

Barry Lopez, author of *Arctic Dreams* and *Embrace Fearlessly the Burning World* and one of the world's preeminent nature writers, once wrote, "Wilderness represents a gene pool, vital for the resiliency of plants and animals." You and I may arrive at this tree to observe its wide branches, a spreading crown, and a magnificent girth. We may embrace its longevity and admire its dendroidal permanence. But we may miss something: its mighty stand has been against nature's forces, not those of humankind. In so doing it has grown to its own dimensions, its own unique resiliency.

And yet this tree, like many in the Sierras, is under stress—stressors compounded by the pervasiveness of climate change. Expansive decades of drought, more intense than those of previous centuries, are the result of a persistent rise in ambient temperatures. This in turn increases evapotranspiration (evaporation from planet leaves and from the ground), which makes less water available to a wide range of plant life.

Drought-stressed trees eventually develop numerous health issues, including a proliferation of burrowing bark beetles that chew their way into the phloem (the inner bark of a tree) without any resistance by pitch, the first line of defense for a tree. Those beetles often create hollows and lay their eggs, which eventually hatch into larvae that create their own entrances into the phloem, a continuous and deadly act that slowly but ever so surely shuts down the tree's circulation. So, too, does climate change affect insect populations such that their numbers may increase dramatically to the point where even healthy long-lived trees, like the Bennett Juniper, meet with their deadly progress. According to figures from the National Park Service, the rate of tree mortality across the western United States doubled between 1955 and 2007. Concurrently, California lost approximately 142 million trees between 2012 and 2018 because of various environmental stressors associated with climate change. So far, the Bennett has escaped the encroaching wrath.

Poets may write long sonnets about the Bennett's beauty, writers may pen engaging adjectives about its age, and readers may admire its prosperous existence. Beyond lyrics or celebrations, however, this tree is a vibrant exemplar of biological integrity and an organism that clearly defines its environment. Some may even argue that it is a fortunate survivor of natural forces and biological circumstances. Yet, to this day, it remains a hallmark of wilderness, a tribute to nature, and a sublime celebration of time.

So too, is it a testament to wonder.

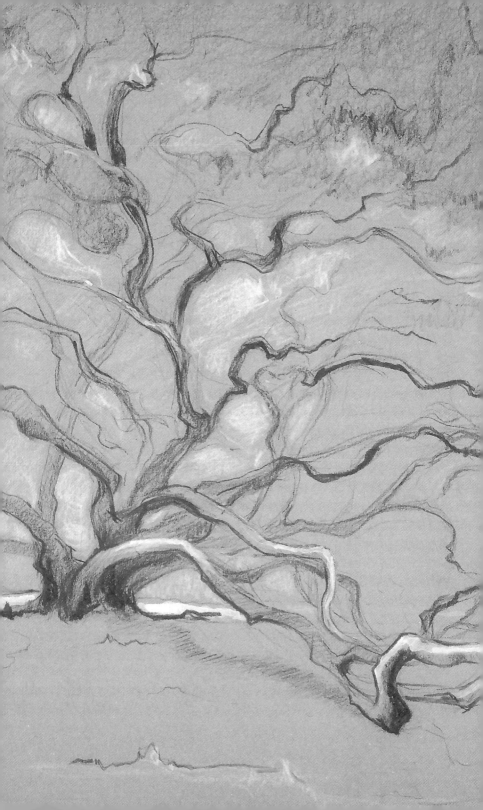

CHAPTER 10

Sight to See

Common name: Southern Live Oak

Scientific binomial: *Quercus virginiana*

Age: ~1,200 years

Location: Mandeville, Louisiana

820 CE, Khwarazm, Greater Iran

Generations of high school freshmen have vilified and cursed him for what he foisted on their secondary education. While his name is often unknown to those students, they often remember his impact on their education long after championship football games, celebratory proms, and graduations.

Muḥammad ibn Mūsā al-Khwārizmī (ca. 780 CE–850 CE) was the originator of algebra. In about 820 CE, he wrote a book entitled *The Compendious Book on Calculation by Completion and Balancing.* He filled it with examples with applications to a wide range of problems. It was also the first book to use the word "algebra," a term derived from one of the basic operations with equations (*al-jabr,* meaning "the setting of broken bones," refers to adding a number to both sides of an equation to consolidate or cancel terms, while mangling the name al-Khwārizmī gives us our term "algorithm").

Al-Khwārizmī's method of solving linear and quadratic equations worked by reducing an equation to one of six standard forms: squares equal roots ($ax^2 = bx$), squares equal number ($ax^2 = c$), roots equal number ($bx = c$), squares and roots equal number

$(ax^2 + bx = c)$, squares and number equal roots $(ax^2 + c = bx)$, and roots and number equal squares $(bx + c = ax^2)$. Algebra, *al-jabr*, is the process of removing negative units, roots, and squares from an equation by adding the same quantity to each side. You might want to test your own algebraic proficiency by solving the following word problem: Miranda picked some oranges from one of the trees in her parent's orchard. If she subtracted 17 from the number of oranges she picked and divided the remainder by 3, she gets 13. How many oranges did she pick? (The answer is at the end of the chapter.)

In later years, mathematical scholars such as Victor J. Katz, Florian Cajori, and Carl Boyer would identify al-Khwārizmī's algebra as one of the most significant cornerstones of the sciences. By comparison, the discovery that trees have been extant on the earth for roughly four hundred million years, and that we have the fossils to prove their early and prolonged existence, may also be considered as one of the cornerstones of arboreal research. At the very least, it changes our conception about the longevity of trees on this planet.

Algebra was one of the most momentous advances made by Arabic mathematics, a true and explicit object of mathematical study, and a straightforward and elementary exposition of the solution of equations. Al-Khwārizmī altered the study of mathematics as much as he altered the education of first-year high school students.

820 CE, Mandeville, Louisiana

A tiny sprout pushed its way through loose soil and the detritus of crumbled leaves to present itself to the world 7,297 miles (11,743 km) west of al-Khwārizmī's birthplace. Inconspicuous, it soaked in the radiant sunshine, absorbed vital nutrients, and readied itself for a life most magnificent. Eventually, it would grow into a massive organism, one that dominated the landscape and one that would dominate minds.

Indigenous peoples, originally nomadic, roamed this rough, yet vibrant land, stalking grand herds of mammals. In time these natives settled down and established settlements, where they farmed beans, maize, sunflowers, and squash. Theirs was a patriarchal society with the men in charge of hunting, fishing, building, and defending the tribal communities. Women produced clothes and utensils, cared for children, and planted crops. By the time Europeans arrived in the sixteenth century, there were approximately ten thousand Indigenous peoples across the land we now know as Louisiana. These people represented six distinct linguistic groups: Caddo, Chitimachan, Tunican, Natchez, Muskogean, and Atakapa. They often lived in wood-framed houses thatched with palmetto branches or constructed of grass. They made clothes of bark, feathers, and hides complimented by an arrangement of body ornaments. The dead were honored with burial mounds preceded by grand celebrations full of dance and song. Although the tribes had different religious traditions, they gave agency to nature and the land. In respect, they seldom took without giving back.

Present Day
It is a sylvan octopus embraced by time. Limbs askew, extended appendages locked in woody permanence, it stands proud and imposing against the brilliance of a vast Louisiana sky. It does not move, but it moves all who gaze upon its magnificence. This tree has survived centuries of torrential rainstorms, ferocious windstorms, and tumultuous hurricanes.

When regarded from afar, this stately individual stands out against the horizon, surrounded by smaller trees sprinkled nearby. Its appendages soar toward the sky, arch toward the ground, and loop back again to the sun. This mélange of limbs is both its defining feature as well as a persistence against the devastating tirades of hurricanes and storms. It is a vigorous and classic southern live oak, *Quercus virginiana*, one with a height of sixty-eight feet (20.7 m), an overall circumference of 39.8 feet (12.1 m), and a canopy spread of 139 feet (42.4 m), or slightly more than the length of three pickleball courts laid end to end.

Epiphytes such as Spanish moss frequently adorn the branches of live oaks such as the Seven Sisters Oak.

The term "live oak" embraces several different species in the genus *Quercus*, of which *Quercus virginiana* may be the best known. Live oaks are also known as evergreen oaks, to distinguish them from deciduous oak trees. Southern live oaks replace their leaves over a period of several weeks in the spring. In the winter months, a time when other varieties of oak are leafless and dormant, *Quercus* maintains its greenery and is thus considered "live." Acorns produced by these trees fall in autumn, where several varieties of birds such as turkeys, mallards, and sapsuckers and mammals such as black bears, squirrels, and deer feast on them.

Live oaks are some of the most iconic trees of the South, particularly with long strands of Spanish moss (*Tillandsia usneoides*) hugging their branches and draped from sweeping limbs that plunge to the ground and then up again. The Seven Sisters Oak, as this massive tree is called, sports this creeping epiphyte, moss that congregates on the bark of a tree and can often become dense enough to shade the tree's foliage in addition to increasing its wind loading—that is, the stresses and tensions the wind transmits to a tree. The moss is nonparasitic, absorbing water through its surface via rainfall and high levels of humidity. Spanish moss absorbs carbon dioxide only at night or shortly after daytime rainstorms, unlike most plants, which absorb carbon dioxide during the day that they then use for photosynthesis. Major storms often strip the moss from branches and scatter it about the perimeter of the tree. Over a period of several years, the moss will repopulate a tree, only to be torn off again in later major storms.

The tree is called the Seven Sisters Oak. At one time, local people thought that several trees had grown together, but in 1976, federal foresters inspected the tree and proved that it had a single root system.

Unlike other trees in this book, the Seven Sisters Oak is located on private property, a two-story home at 200 Fountain Street in the Lewisburg neighborhood of Mandeville, Louisiana. Just a brief stroll from the north shore of Lake Pontchartrain, it presents a stunning silhouette, an impressive figure, and a cinematic icon for photographers from across the country and around the world. Out of respect for the owners, visitors should keep a courteous distance.

The Seven Sisters Oak was originally named Doby's Seven Sisters because the owner who first named the tree, Carole Hendry Doby, was one of seven sisters, and the tree was located on what was then Doby property. This designation was probably a way of honoring and preserving the family legacy by extending it a particularly long-lived tree. It eventually came to be called the Seven Sisters Oak, although the reason for the name change has never been stated. Most significant is that this tree was elevated to the rank of reigning president of the Live Oak Society in 1968.

According to William Guion, who has researched and photographed oaks throughout Louisiana since 1985, Edwin

Stephens, first president of the Southwestern Louisiana Institute, now the University of Louisiana at Lafayette, wrote an article entitled "I Saw in Louisiana a Live Oak Growing" which was published in 1934 in the *Louisiana Conservation Review*. Patterned after a poem by Walt Whitman, Stephens's piece celebrated the unique beauty of this distinctive species of oak. Stephens spent years observing, collecting data, and photographing live oaks, with a particular focus on the oldest and largest. Stephens envisioned the live oak as a significant cultural, historical, and artistic symbol for Louisiana, even arguing that its Latin name should have been *Quercus louisiana* rather than *Quercus virginiana* simply because of the rich abundance of live oaks throughout the Pelican State. In his article, Stephens also advocated for the creation of a professional organization that would protect and preserve the oldest living members of *Quercus virginiana* throughout their range.

The purpose of the Live Oak Society is to promote the culture, distribution, preservation, and appreciation of southern live oaks. According to the bylaws of the organization, only one human can be a member of the organization at any one time, and that person is responsible for registering and recording all the Live Oak Society's other members, namely, the trees. To become a member of the Society, a live oak is required to have a girth, or waistline, of eight feet (2.4 m) or greater. The Live Oak Society began with forty-three members and now boasts over 8,800 members in fourteen states.

The Society's first president was the Locke Breaux Oak in Taft, Louisiana, which lost its life in the late 1960s to air and groundwater pollution. Shortly after, the Seven Sisters Oak was formally and officially inaugurated as the Society's second president, honored for its dominating size and exquisite beauty. John McKeithen, governor of Louisiana, was one of the honored guests at the induction ceremony. Witnesses reported that this celebratory event included, among other festivities, several musical selections from the US Marine Corps Band. The tunes accompanied a troupe of ballet dancers who pirouetted around the base of the titan, much to the delight of onlookers. At the conclusion of the celebration, each of the attendees received a wooden "coin" stamped with a likeness of the tree.

Curious to know more about the Live Oak Society and its president, I contacted Coleen Perilloux Landry, the chairperson and only human member of the Society since 2000. She told me that the overall mission of the Society was to promote, preserve and protect the Live Oak tree. Throughout its existence, the Society has negotiated and fought with big agencies such as the Corps of Engineers and State and Federal Highway Departments to save live oaks that were slated for removal. The agencies, for the most part, cooperated when the Society showed them how to tunnel under a tree for a drainage project, how to move a tree to another location, and in some cases how to reroute a highway. As Landry pointed out, it was one of the Society's missions to staunchly support each of its members, irrespective of location or age.

Landry's embrace of this ceremonious tree was evident when she shared part of its history. She told me that in late spring and early summer, when rainfall averages rise to five to seven inches a month, the nearby Mississippi River often overflows its banks, the excess water emptying into nearby Lake Pontchartrain. Quite often, the lake, two blocks from the Seven Sisters Oak, spills over its banks and floods the area in and around the tree. As a result, Landry noted, the now deceased first president of the Society and the living second president have both absorbed the waters of the Mississippi River.

Landry recounted that people from all over the world come to see Seven Sisters Oak not just for its sprawling elegance but also because of how it has withstood forces of nature that would topple lesser trees. She pointed out, that over several centuries, this particular live oak has endured and survived at least ten major hurricanes with little damage. Recent events include Hurricane Ida in 2021, with maximum sustained winds of 150 mph (241 km/h), Hurricane Katrina in 2005 with maximum winds of 175 mph (282 km/h), and Hurricane Lili in 2002 with wind gusts reaching 120 mph (193 km/h).

Live oaks are resilient to hurricane wind forces with only minor to moderate damage. In the aftermath of one expansive hurricane, 30 percent of live oaks were undamaged, 50 percent had bent or broken limbs, 16 percent were heavily defoliated, 5 percent had broken tops, 2 percent had broken stems, and less than 3 percent had been uprooted or knocked down. Storms often do little more than rip off leaves and small branches. For the most part, trees typically escape relatively unscathed.

E. J. Dennis, a live oak specialist and the caretaker for the Seven Sisters Oak since 2006, shares that live oaks have such strength because they are considerably broader than they are tall, with wide canopies and an extensive root system. Their branches grow in multiple directions and at multiple heights, factors that also make them particularly resilient to the force of storms blowing in from the Gulf of Mexico. Form follows function in assuring their extended and ancient lives.

A significant contributor to live oaks' longevity is due to their adaptability to a range of environments, including acidic, alkaline, loamy, moist, sandy, and clay soils. While these trees prefer regular access to moisture, they do have some drought tolerance. Initially, they grow rapidly, although their growth rate declines with age. Sometimes they will reach an expanded trunk circumference of thirty-five feet (10.7 m) or more, which suggest that the tree has been alive for more than six hundred years.

Kim D. Coder of the School of Forest Resources at the University of Georgia notes that lives oaks typically have a maximum expected life span of approximately four hundred years. However, accurately determining their longevity is a real challenge because of the hardness of the wood and the presence of decay columns in older specimens. In the absence of accurate measurement records, it is not unusual for many long-standing live oaks to have "guesstimates" about their overall age and historical record.

Known for their incredibly strong and durable wood, live oaks were once the preferred tree for shipbuilding. Their wood was so valuable that the US Navy once maintained its own live oak forest. The government established the Naval Live Oaks Reservation, near Gulf Breeze, Florida, in 1828 under authorization from President John Quincy Adams. Beginning operations on January 1, 1829, it was under the supervision of Henry Marie Brackenridge, considered the country's first federal forester. The purpose of the reservation was to provide sufficient quantities of live oak wood for the construction of US Navy ships in nearby Pensacola. The yard was in continuous operation from the 1820s through the time of the Civil War.

Some of the lumber used in the construction of the naval frigate USS *Constitution* was live oak. During the War of 1812, when British warships fired cannonballs at *Constitution*, they literally bounced off the sturdy hull, which is why the vessel has long been affectionately referred to as "Old Ironsides." In 1926, during the reconstruction of the *Constitution*, shipbuilders used live oak from the Pensacola region once again for some of its repairs.

Near the end of the Civil War, most Navy ships were built of iron, and the need for wood for them declined precipitously. The former Reservation was subsequently converted to a 1,300 acre (526 ha) nature preserve, now maintained by Gulf Islands National Seashore.

There is another well-known and well-visited live oak, this one located on Johns Island near Charleston, South Carolina. It stands as one of the most heralded live oaks ever, and, although it is "only" four hundred to five hundred years old, it is revered. Known as the Angel Oak, it was named for Justus Angel and his wife, Martha Waight Tucker Angel, who took possession of the land on which the tree stands in 1810. The tree is one of the most popular attractions in the Charleston area, receiving more than 400,000 visitors every year. Standing 66.5 feet (20.3 m) tall, measuring twenty-eight feet (8.5 m) in circumference, and producing shade that covers 17,200 square feet (1,598 sq m), Angel Oak is the 210th tree registered with the Live Oak Society. This specimen, like its Louisiana cousin, has survived the ravages of hurricanes, the shock of lightning strikes, the severity of thundering storms, and the onslaught of decay. It has come to symbolize all live oaks with its vibrancy, fortitude, and resilience, just like its cousin to the southwest.

Growing up in and around the chilled waters of the Pacific Ocean, I was in constant awe of the myriad sea creatures that inhabited the world beneath Southern California waves. From sea anemones to leopard sharks, stinging jellyfish to migrating humpback whales, I dove into and swam through a transcendent and liquid zoo. At times, I would enter the mystical world of cephalopods, which include octopuses, squids, nautiluses, and cuttlefish, many-armed creatures whose fossil record extends back in time some five hundred million years. Indeed, these are creatures most ancient, most old. They have been around for longer than 99 percent of all the animals that have ever existed on the planet. They have been preserved in rock and captured by aquariums. Their longevity is forever. They are beyond years.

Octopuses have eight arms. Cuttlefish and squids have eight arms and two tentacles. Adult nautili have between sixty and ninety tentacles, depending on the species. They are diverse, and they fascinate us with their rhythmic movements and fluid motions, dancing beneath the waves. Their supple limbs entrance us with that ancient choreography.

So it is with the Seven Sisters Oak, a "woody octopus" that gambols against the reflective light left behind from a summer storm, a grand arboreal specimen waltzing through a panoply of climatological challenges, and a botanical wonder that bows but does not break when fierce and angry winds challenge its longevity. It has stood against all manner of forces and survived quite well. It is testimonial to endurance and longevity.

As to the algebra problem:

Let x = number of oranges Miranda picked.

1. $\dfrac{x-17}{3} = 13$

2. $\dfrac{(3)\,x-17}{3} = 13\,(3)$

3. $x - 17 = 39$

4. $x - 17 + 17 = 39 + 17$

5. $x = 56$

Miranda picked fifty-six oranges.

In Celebration of Old Trees

It was early summer 2015. I had paused along the Lady Bird Johnson Grove Loop in Redwood National Park. Before me stood a giant tree that had maintained its station for centuries. I began my visual journey in the splendor of its verdant canopy and slowly brought my eyes down a massive and striated trunk. As my vision reached the forest floor, I noticed a wedge of ancient history: an irregular shard of weathered wood several feet to the left of the tree's base. The fragment was slightly larger than my index finger, lying amid a cluster of well-shaded ferns.

I picked it up. While holding it in my hand, I felt a presence and a communion, a story to be experienced and shared. It was a morsel of time, a fragment of endurance, and a testament to age. The tree from which it came may have been logged in another century or shattered by a thunderous lightning bolt decades before my discovery, but this remnant was a reminder that a titan once stood and prospered in this arena. It was a signal, perhaps an invitation, to discover its heritage. It became a spark for this book.

That fragment of timber, throughout the ensuing years, was also a token of individuals seen and species experienced in my ventures to search for, and learn about, ancient trees. It was also an emblem of the high mountain ranges, humid swamps, coastal ranges, rural enclaves, and remote prairies I traversed in my search for botanical wonders that expanded my concept of longevity and heightened my awareness of magnificent forests. I returned it to its place. A photograph of it, now on a corner of my desk, is constant inspiration for the wonders of ancient trees, a reminder of both beauty and truth.

Trees, and the forests they inhabit, are members of a vast and complex ecosystem that sustains the planet as much as they sustain our lives. They are sonnets upon the Earth, a celebration of life in all its splendor. They harbor a complexity of life forms— mammals, birds, amphibians, reptiles, fish, and, of course, the humans who wander their trails and explore their dynamics. They provide us with life-sustaining oxygen, a bounty of food, clean water, a vast array of medicines, and places of retreat and contemplation. They are reservoirs of life as much as they are biological guardians.

    Trees are essential to the survival of all forms of life. Collectively, they absorb approximately 20 percent of greenhouse gas emissions, they offer sanctuary to enormous numbers of creatures, they regulate global temperatures across a range of climatic zones, they provide humans with resources necessary to create dwellings, clothing, and food resources, and they beautify our environments with their grace and greenery. Their influence is a constant, both historically and biologically. Their presence a necessity.

    This is no more so than with trees that have achieved exceptionally long lives, trees that have expanded our respect for lives well lived, trees that have opened our eyes to the mysteries of nature. These are trees of magnificence. They stand apart from the familiar; they are beacons of resiliency and determination. We know them via the science of dendrochronology, dating them whether alive or dead to the precise year they formed. The accumulation of that data offers scientists important insights about climate patterns, atmospheric conditions, and geological events during various periods in Earth's history.

My arboreal adventures among the long-lived sequoias in central California, the venerable specimens in the Ancient Bristlecone Pine Forest, a prehistoric and inconspicuous Palmer's oak, a multibranched aspen tree in south-central Utah, the languid realm of legendary bald cypresses along the Black River, a singular juniper tree standing resolute and determined on a scrubby hillside, the majestic redwood trees along a narrow strip of geography in northern California, and the dance of a live oak that has survived powerful and unforgiving winds for centuries, were not only voyages of discovery but also, in so many ways, entrees into a world often unseen, yet similarly eye-opening. Their lives, measured in rings, are a reminder that nature has much to share and much to appreciate. We need only step outside and look into the woods.

It was late winter, and a congregation of dark clouds approached from the south as I took my afternoon walk along the border of a public golf course adjacent to our neighborhood. After about a mile, I met up with an acquaintance walking his dog. We both stopped and exchanged the usual pleasantries. He soon inquired about the status of this book and what I was learning during its composition. I shared some of my adventures as well as discoveries. He then asked a most penetrating question: "What is the importance of ancient trees?"

It was a topic that lurked in the background of every narrative, a persistent query tucked between the paragraphs and shadowing the sometimes complicated research. Why are these trees important—and why should we care? The response to my neighbor was, I hoped, both reverent and considerate.

In so many ways, ancient trees are messengers from the past, historical storytellers of time and place and biological circumstances. Old trees harbor deep arboreal secrets, sometimes teased out by scientists and sometimes locked within their cambium for long centuries. It is those tales that, quite often, command our attention. It is the embrace of those accounts that furthers their importance. And for that there are many champions.

The Archangel Ancient Tree Archive, headquartered in Copemish, Michigan, seeks to ensure the survival of ancient trees through a three-stage process. Their focus is on (1) the scientific cloning of the oldest and largest trees in existence; (2) the creation of the world's first "super grove" of cloned coast redwoods and giant sequoias in Oregon; and (3) the replanting of old trees to form an archive, or a living library, of Champion trees. According to AATAs Mission Statement, preserving "old growth trees through traditional and advanced horticultural propagation [allows us] to replace the natural filter systems of our water and air, to fight global warming caused climate change, and protect our freshwater ecosystem to restore the health of our planet." In short, the AATA believes that ancient trees are critical to the natural health of all organisms, now and well into the future. The organization's cofounder, David Milarch, puts the importance of its work in clear context when he says, "We saved these trees, and now they will save the world."

American Forests also puts a premium on ancient trees through its National Champion Trees Project. In place for almost a hundred years, this campaign empowers citizens to locate the largest living specimens of America's trees and, by extension, those that have achieved old ages. In its early years, the project's goal was to engage the public in forestry activities, essentially a national hunt to discover the largest living specimens of select tree species. However, the program has since shifted its focus. Now the intent is to help people aid in the prevention of biodiversity loss, increase awareness of the ecosystem services of big trees, and foster a desire to protect and preserve these tall timbers for future generations. This most successful venture stirs enormous interest in trees of all ages, creating advocates for the preservation of organisms essential to human health and well-being. In essence, the public's involvement in identifying big trees fosters its engagement in ensuring the trees' long lives, as well as their continuing contributions.

In 2022–2023, a signature court case took place in British Columbia, Canada, one that would ultimately be decided by ancient trees. The Indigenous community of the Nuchatlaht First Nation had filed a lawsuit against the province, arguing that it had rights and title to approximately seventy-eight square miles (20,000 ha) of land on Nootka Island, just off the west coast of Vancouver Island. The Canadian government contended that it owned the land and that the Nuchatlaht had no continuous connection to the territory. To make their case, the Nuchatlaht needed to prove their occupancy of the land before and up to 1846, which is when England gained sovereignty over British Columbia in a treaty with the United States. The Nuchatlaht used, as evidence, thousand-year-old red cedar trees that demonstrated the long cultural practice of bark harvesting. Generations of Nuchatlaht have used red cedar bark to make medicines, fishing tools, and clothing. Scientists working in the area were able to identify about 2,500 culturally modified trees, each with lobes healed around harvested bark. That healing process creates grooves that can be accurately dated back for several centuries. For the Nuchatlaht, as well as for other First Nations, the importance of ancient trees may well be in their preservation of cultural traditions and, by extension, their provincial claims to ancestral lands. As a result, these trees help ensure the sovereignty of Indigenous peoples and the maintenance of Aboriginal rights. It's a tall order, but these old-timers are certainly up to the task.

An article in a 2022 issue of *Smithsonian Magazine* heralded the discovery of old-growth trees throughout previously unexamined New England forests. Through the persistence of a most passionate forester, one Bob Leverett, amazing insights have been uncovered relative to ancient trees and their influence upon the land. The author of the piece makes a case for ancient forests as systems as well as for their uninterrupted ecological cycles over time. The overriding thesis is that these old forests sustain myriad sets of biological processes, complex, interconnected systems of continuous renewal. For example, Leverett demonstrated how older trees accumulate far more carbon later in their life cycles than had previously been thought. His research clearly established that trees accumulate about 75 percent of their carbon after fifty years of age, giving credence to the construct that ancient forests may have more of an impact in mitigating the impact of climate change than would, say, an emphasis on reforestation. Leverett's work is supported by a 2017 study that concluded that if the world's forests were just left alone, by 2100 they would capture enough carbon to offset years' worth of global fossil-fuel emissions. What becomes clear is that humans have an ever-present duty to protect old forests, not just because of their beauty or age but also for their importance to the planet.

Another article also released in early 2022, this one in the journal *Nature Plants*, looked at the effects of old trees on the flora around them. In the words of the scientist authors, "these rare, ancient trees prove to be vital to a forest's long term adaptive capacity, substantially broadening the temporal span of the population's overall genetic diversity." In short, the experiences of old trees, genetically speaking, can be passed along to younger trees, thus ensuring their potential longevity. Unsurprisingly, the scientists proved that ancient trees offer shelter and protection for endangered species and, as Bob Leverett discovered, they are much better at soaking up carbon than their younger contemporaries. The significance of these discoveries was underlined by a prophetic statement near the end of the article, "Once you [lose] old and ancient trees, we lose the genetic and physiological legacy that they contain forever, as well as the unique habitat for nature conservation."

The importance of ancient trees often supersedes their beauty as well as their longevity. Their permanence upon the earth is a clue as to what we consider important, what we value and support. It may be a bit of overstatement to say that our existence, our very survival, may be dependent, in large measure, on the natural biological processes of trees—youngsters and ancients alike. But it bears consideration that trees, ancient trees especially, are a most necessary element of biological existence and permanence. Consider what we may lose were they all to disappear. The planet would, most assuredly, change, and exponentially.

I suppose the next time I meet my neighbor on a late afternoon stroll, we will have much to discuss, and much to share, about the importance of ancient trees. Especially while standing near the copse of white oaks (*Quercus alba*) guarding the seventh fairway.

"The forest is not only something to be understood, but also something to be felt." So said Joan Maloof, the founder and driving force of the Old-Growth Forest Network (OGFN), a network of long-standing forests throughout the United States to which visitors can travel to experience ancient trees. OGFN's goal is to locate and designate at least one protected forest in every county in the United States that can sustain a native forest. It estimates that to be approximately 2,370 out of 3,140 total counties. To accomplish that goal, OGFN works to identify old growth forests, ensure their protection, and inform the public of specific forest locations. The group's ultimate mission is to create not only a network of forests but also an alliance of people who care about forests.

Underscoring OGFN's mission are some staggering statistics: less than 5 percent of the original forests in states west of the Mississippi and less than 1 percent of the original forests east of the Mississippi still stand.

I caught up with Joan Maloof on a chilly spring afternoon just before Earth Day 2022. When I asked her to define the reasoning for the Old-Growth Forest Network, she was adamant about the need to bring older forests to the general public's attention. She offered several reasons, including how beautiful they are, their biodiversity, their support for many other living organisms, and their importance for our climate. When I queried her about the long-range implications of OGFN's mission, she responded that if folks live anywhere near a forested part of the country there will most likely be an old-growth forest within it, one that can always be visited and one that will never be cut down. She went on to emphasize that old-growth forests also offer youngsters an introduction to most vibrant ecosystems. The result is a relationship that will make them want to preserve older forests for their generation and the next.

Maloof went on to say that humans have a tendency to manipulate the Earth. That is, humans cut their lawns, put in roads, plow fields, or mow crops. "But in a forest, you're seeing what the earth wants to create," she said.

If you don't have a sprawling forest of redwoods, a tannin-infused river of bald cypresses, a nine-thousand-year-old aspen tree, or a grove of ancient bristlecone pines near where you live, consider communion with an old-growth forest. You can easily locate one nearby via www.oldgrowthforest.net. At this writing, OGFN has dedicated more than 175 forests as it continues to expand its outreach across the United States.

As readers are aware, forests throughout the world are under duress. Vast tracts fall every day for commercial greed. For example, the Amazon rainforest, often considered as the "Lungs" of the Earth, is losing approximately ten thousand acres (4,406 ha) per day, primarily to illegal logging. This elimination results in an increase of global temperatures as well as a critical loss of wildlife habitats. Large-scale deforestation also negatively affects hydrological cycles resulting in rampant soil erosion, extreme flooding, and enormous population shifts.

The ominous specter of climate change looms large when forests are cut down. The lack of a robust assembly of trees to sequester carbon affects the life cycles and survival rates of numerous life forms. Greenhouse gas emissions, particularly from logging enterprises in concert with an increase in global and national wildfires, spiral upward. As noted earlier, the march of rising temperatures worldwide also results in a persistent migration of both plants and animals into new territories and unfamiliar ecosystems. Life is changed.

Deforestation and climate change also affect ancient trees. Their lives, too, are challenged, their vitality compromised. Yet we have province and inclination to make a difference in the longevity of all trees, irrespective of their years. There is much we can do to ensure long lives for our botanical neighbors so that we measure their existence not in memories but rather in long expanses of resiliency and determination. First, take time to regularly step into a forest, wander its trails, and pause before its inhabitants. Gaze up into the canopies, observe the scramble of wildlife, and admire the interactions constantly taking place amongst long branches and broad trunks. Get to know a forest or a grove of trees as evolutionary partners and environmental neighbors. Feel the vibrancy and share the experience, many times, with children. Knowing a nearby forest gives you a door into all forests, those just beginning and those most ancient.

Second, examine the agencies and organizations working to ensure the survival of ancient trees. The Save the Redwoods League, Friends of Pando, Bald Cypress Consortium, Mother Lode Land Trust, and Sempervirens Fund, along with other "ancient tree groups," have numerous opportunities for volunteers along with a persistent need for financial support to do their work. These organizations also have a library of documents, brochures, books, online resources, and information for anyone interested in influencing the ongoing preservation of old trees.

Third, consider joining or contributing to long-standing environmental groups such as the Sierra Club, Nature Conservancy, National Park Foundation, Wilderness Society, and National Forest Foundation, to name only a few. Many of these groups have regional and local affiliates that welcome new members, both individuals and families. The work they do is critical to the success of all forests and their inhabitants.

True, there is much work to do to preserve forests. But on the positive side, we have been moving in the right direction, making necessary strides to ensure the longevity of forests and trees across the United States. Witness the Nature Conservancy and its purchase and protection of more than 125 million acres (50,506,000 ha) of land. Imagine the long-range impact of the Save the Redwoods League, which over the past one hundred years has protected more than 216,000 acres (87,410 ha) of redwood forests and helped create sixty-six redwood parks and reserves. Think of the Friends of Pando and its determination to educate the public, support numerous research and preservation efforts, and inspire long-term stewardship of the world's largest tree. Consider the efforts of American Forests and its vision of a world in which the significant environmental, societal, and economic benefits of forests are fully realized and equitably available to all people. In working with and supporting these groups, we too can help ensure the vitality and preservation of trees everywhere. In short, you and I and all our neighbors have both reason and rationale to protect ancient trees and conserve their future.

In the years of my life, I have traveled many forests. Each venture has brought me closer to environmental truths and ecological realities. It is an education traced by sylvan footsteps and a constant passion for discovery. As I learned in this odyssey, the experiences of ancient trees are great pauses against the nonstop demands of everyday life. So, too, are they physical sanctuaries offering time for contemplation and consideration, respite and reflection. They are objects of affection as much as they are sentinels of time. We can absorb much in their presence.

In walking through ancient trees, I have every reason to celebrate their lives. I have every hope for their extended existence, their permanence upon the earth. They are unique, ever distinctive.

I invite you, dear reader, to stand among these magnificent specimens, to trod meandering trails, and to touch their timeworn barks. I invite you to experience a vibrant and compelling combination of human wonder and botanical stature. Most important, I invite you to be as one with the ancient forest. You might feel, as I have, a natural celebration of longevity, a responsibility to a timbered world, and a deep communion with great beings. In turn, you will learn much. Reach out.

The trees await.

The Oldest Trees in the World

While this book focuses exclusively on tree species extant in the United States, there are specimens in far-flung geographies that also live long lives. For several of the examples in the following list, the reported age(s) may be more a common and accepted belief than an accurate scientific measurement. The legend and lore of a particular culture shroud many of these trees. Their life story may be part of a long-standing myth or an ancient historical event. That certainly does not make them any less spectacular—it only underscores our scientific curiosity and historical fascination with old-timers.

Common name: Castagna dei Cento Cavalli
Scientific binomial: *Castanea sativa*
Age: 2,000–4,000 years (est.)
Location: Mount Etna, Sicily

This tree, whose Italian name means Chestnut Tree of One Hundred Horses, is the largest and oldest known chestnut tree in the world. Its name comes from a Renaissance legend in which the Queen of Aragon and her retinue of one hundred knights and their horses sought shelter under the spreading arms of the tree during a violent storm.

Common name: Crespin Ficus
Scientific binomial: *Ficus retusa* Linn

Age: ~1,000 years (est.)
Location: Milan, Italy

This ten-foot (3 m)-tall evergreen lives in the Crispi Bonsai Museum
in the world's largest bonsai pot. Often cited as the oldest existing bonsai tree in the world, this meticulously crafted tree show-
cases a network of dense aerial roots and an exquisitely
balanced profile.

Common name: El Arbol del Tule
Scientific binomial: *Taxodium mucronatum*
Age: 1,433–1,600 years (est.)
Location: Santa María del Tule, Oaxaca, Mexico

Classified as one of the oldest cypress trees in the world, the Tule tree's
overall age is based primarily on its growth rate. This specimen rises to a
height of 116 feet (35 m) and has a circumference of nearly 138 feet (42 m).
Locals consider its site a sacred location.

Common name: Elia Vouvon
Scientific binomial: *Olea europaea*
Age: 4,000+ years (est.)
Location: Ano Vouves, Crete

Located on Crete, this specimen is one of the oldest trees still producing
olives. The Greek government declared it a protected national monument
in 2009.

Common name: Fortingall Yew
Scientific binomial: *Taxus baccata*
Age: 2,000–3,000 years (est.)
Location: Perthshire, Scotland

Located in the graveyard of the village of Fortingall, this tree is one of the oldest in Great Britain. At one time, the trunk of this tree measured fifty-two feet (15.9 m) wide. However, it has since split into several smaller stems.

Common name: Gran Abuelo
Scientific binomial: *Fitzroya cupressoides*
Age: 3,651 years
Location: Alerce Costero National Park, Chile

This specimen is native to the Andes Mountains of South America. Some botanists consider the species to be some of oldest living trees in the world, second only to the bristlecone pines of California. The age of the Gran Abuelo was determined through an analysis of its growth rings.

Common name: Gümeli Porsuğu
Scientific binomial: *Taxus baccata*
Age: 4,115 years (est.)
Location: Zonguldak District, Turkey

Although its age is a scientific estimate, this yew tree, most certainly, began its life sometime during the Bronze Age (3300 BCE–1200 BCE). This was a time when humans first began creating tools and weapons of metal.

Common name: Houkisugi
Scientific binomial: *Cryptomeria japonica*
Age: 2,000 years (est.)
Location: Kanagawa Prefecture, Japan

A Japanese cedar tree, Houkisugi is one of the oldest and tallest trees in Japan. Standing 148 feet (45 m) high, it has an overall circumference of 39 feet (11.9 m).

Common name: Huon Pine
Scientific binomial: *Lagarostrobos franklinii*
Age: 10,500+ years
Location: Mount Read, Tasmania, Australia

A concentration of Huon pines in excess of 10,500 years old inhabits
Mount Read in western Tasmania. Each of the trees is a genetically
identical male that has reproduced vegetatively. Although no single tree
in this stand is of that age, the stand itself as a single organism has
existed that long.

Common name: Jaya Sri Maha Bodhi
Scientific binomial: *Ficus religiosa*
Age: 2,307 years
Location: Mahamewna, Anuradhapura, Sri Lanka

It has been recorded that Sanghamitra, the daughter of King Ashoka,
brought from India a branch of the sacred bodhi tree, a kind of fig, under
which Buddha attained enlightenment. As a result, this specimen has
tremendous historical and religious relevance.

Common name: Jōmon Sugi
Scientific binomial: *Cryptomeria japonica*
Age: 2,170 to 7,200 years (est.)
Location: Yakushima, Japan

This tree is somewhat controversial, since there seems to be little
consensus as to its true age. Nevertheless, it is considered to be the oldest
and largest cryptomeria tree in the world. Its location is a UNESCO World
Heritage Site.

Common name: Kayano Ōsugi, The Great Sugi of Kayano
Scientific binomial: *Cryptomeria japonica*

Age: 2,300 years (est.)
Location: Ishikawa Prefecture, Japan

Measuring thirty-eight feet (11.5 m) in circumference, this tree is one of four sugi (Japanese cedar) trees considered sacred by the residents of Yamanaka Onsen. Its reported age was estimated in 1928.

Common name: King's Lomatia
Scientific binomial: *Lomatia tasmanica*
Age: ~43,600 years
Location: Southwestern Tasmania

Individual plants of this species are either shrub-like or short trees. *L. tasmanica* is a clonal organism: when a branch falls, it eventually grows new roots, establishing a new plant that is genetically identical to its parent. With only a single population, it is an endangered species. Scientists have dated its fossilized leaves to about 43,600 years ago.

Common name: Koca Katran
Scientific binomial: *Cedrus libani*
Age: 2,000+ years (est.)
Location: Antalya Province, Turkey

This tree stands eighty-two feet (25 m) tall and measures twenty-seven feet (8 m) in circumference. As such, it is one of the tallest and oldest trees in Turkey. Its name translates to "Big Old Cedar." Prized for their scent, the "cedars of Lebanon," of which this is one, are frequently mentioned in the Old Testament as a symbol of wealth and power.

Common name: Llangernyw Yew
Scientific binomial: *Taxus baccata*

Age: 4,000+ years (est.)
Location: Llangernyw, North Wales

This incredible yew resides on the grounds of St. Diegan's Church in the Welsh hamlet of Llangernyw. In 2002, in celebration of the golden jubilee of Queen Elizabeth II, the Tree Council (UK) designated it one of 50 Great British Trees.

Common name: Old Tjikko
Scientific binomial: *Picea abies*
Age: 9,550 years
Location: Fulufjället Mountains, Sweden

Geologist Leif Kullman discovered this tree in 2008 and named it after his deceased dog. Standing only sixteen feet (4.8 m) tall, it has survived the brutal winters of Sweden. The tree is a clone that keeps regenerating new branches and trunks while maintaining much of its root system.

Common name: Oliveira do Mouchão
Scientific binomial: *Olea europaea*
Age: 3,022–3,350 years
Location: Cascalhos in Mouriscas, Centro, Portugal

As the oldest tree in Portugal, this olive tree has been classified as a "Monumental Tree of Portugal" by the Institute of Conservation of Nature and Forests. It is also one of the oldest living—and still producing—olive trees in the world.

Common name: Panke Baobab
Scientific binomial: *Adansonia digitata*
Age: 2,450 years
Location: Zimbabwe

Listed in the *Guinness Book of World Records* as the oldest hardwood tree
ever, this African baobab reached a distinguished age of at least
2,450 years old when it died in 2011. Since baobabs do not produce wood
that is cross-datable, its age was determined through the use of
radiocarbon dating.

Common name: Patriarca da Floresta
Scientific binomial: *Cariniana legalis*
Age: 3,000 years (est.)
Location: Vassununga National Park, São Paulo, Brazil

The "Patriarch of the Forest" is estimated to be around three thousand
years old. As such, it is one of the oldest conifers in Brazil.

Common name: Sarv-e Abarqu, Zoroastrian Sarv
Scientific binomial: *Cupressus sempervirens*
Age: 4,000+ years (est.)
Location: Yazd Province, Iran

The Sarv-e Abarqu, a kind of cypress, has lived through the beginning of
the Bronze Age in Europe, the initiation of palace civilizations in the
Aegean, and the rise of chariots as war vehicles in the Near East. Many
people consider it the single oldest living thing in Asia.

Common name: Sweet Chestnut
Scientific binomial: *Castanea sativa*
Age: ~1,522 years
Location: Leomil, Norte, Portugal

This relatively short tree, about fifty feet (15 m) tall, can be found in the
north of Portugal. It is a sweet chestnut tree that most likely germinated
around the year 500 CE.

Common name: Tnjri
Scientific binomial: *Platanus orientalis* L.
Age: 2,041 (est.)
Location: Skhtorashen, Armenia

Massive, with a height of 177 feet (54 m) and a circumference of 88 feet (27 m), this is one of the oldest trees in Armenia. The hollow at its base can accommodate more than three dozen people.

Acknowledgments

In this book's journey from a nascent idea almost ten years ago to the bound product you now hold in your hands, I was influenced by a delightful congregation of individuals who contributed immeasurable advice, research, guidance, inspiration, and insights. This ever-expanding group clearly demonstrated that nonfiction books are ultimately dependent on the creative insights and patient hand-holding of friends, colleagues, family members, and a whole lot of strangers. Their unselfish contributions are liberally sprinkled throughout these pages.

First and foremost, my daughter Rebecca gets enormous hugs (and loads of paternal appreciation) for her majestic painting of redwoods that graces the cover of this book. Along with the full-page illustrations that precede each chapter, she has truly captured the essence of ancient trees with an unmatched level of artistic skill and professionalism. My wife, Phyllis, in her vibrant and dynamic presentations of the details of ancient trees within each chapter, also has focused on essential arboreal elements with her usual brand of imagination and precision. She, too, is forever embraced.

Early drafts of the manuscript benefited from editorial suggestions by Vicky Lynott and Susannah Richards, dear friends and fellow authors, who offered necessary guidance and direction on numerous occasions. I am also indebted to transcriber Monica Harris of Living Transcripts, who masterfully transformed every interview into a detailed and accurate document. Her work was laser-perfect and was returned well in advance of due dates. Jack and Linda Sommer, dear friends and fellow vagabonds, are to be celebrated for their constant encouragement and endorsement of this project. They are unparalleled supporters.

I owe an immense intellectual debt to the many scientists, researchers, botanists, and fellow naturalists who generously gave of their time and talents via Zoom interviews, on-site conversations, far too many emails, early morning phone discussions, late night text messages, and innumerable contacts both personal and remote. Not only did they deepen my understanding of matters biological, but they also opened doors of comprehension to share with readers. This book, I hope, honors their commitment to, and work with, ancient trees.

Valerie Trouet (University of Arizona) deserves a standing ovation for her robust contributions to the science of dendrochronology as well as her support of this project. Her enthusiastic words of wisdom clarified significant dendrochronological protocols and promoted a deep appreciation for this fascinating science. Paul Ringgold (Save the Redwoods League) opened doors of understanding about redwoods in general and the essential need for their ongoing and unwavering preservation specifically. Don Hardy (Mahanaim Adventures) was the penultimate guide on our journey down the Black River. His ecological knowledge, fine sense of humor, and historical knowledge made my discovery of bald cypresses an unforgettable experience. David Stahle (University of Arkansas) took valuable time out of a Colorado vacation to discuss the importance of bald cypress trees and the reasons why they have survived all manner of threats and disturbances. Lance Oditt (Friends of Pando) was a gentleman of the highest order. Over numerous Zoom meetings and phone conversations he eagerly shared his passion for the world's largest tree. His expert guidance through and between the branches of Pando was a most delightful journey into the myriad mysteries of nature. A tip of the hat to Richard Walton (Newcastle University, UK) who initially directed me to Lance and his wonderful organization. William Tweed (Sequoia National Park, retired) offered insightful explanations and detailed stories about the history and persistence of some of the most magnificent trees in the world. He opened my eyes and my mind to the magic of these towering specimens. Coleen Landry (Live Oak Society), in the midst of recovering from a recent hurricane, graciously provided me with information into the majesty of most ancient beings. Kristine DeLong (Louisiana State University), in concert with her cat, took time to share one of the most amazing scientific discoveries of the last century; a discovery most critical to our understanding of biological history and the persistent influence of climate change. I am equally indebted to Joan Maloof (Old-Growth Forest Network), not only for her breadth of knowledge about old trees, but clearly for her commitment to their preservation.

So too, is a grand note of appreciation graciously offered to the many folks I met along long and dusty trails, in gift shops and visitor centers, and in the midst of magnificent forests over the past several years. Your names are unknown, but your embrace of these arboreal wonders is most appreciated. Your comments, observations, and delightful remarks while we admired tall timbers or ancient flora continued to propel and inspire me throughout this odyssey.

Working with the crew at Smithsonian Books was not only a professional honor but clearly an incredible literary experience. Their dedication and commitment to quality books and scientific accuracy infused every aspect of this project. They are colleagues and compatriots of the highest order. Director Carolyn Gleason offered valuable editorial comments and suggestions throughout the initial drafts ensuring that the book reflected the highest standards of the Smithsonian Institution. Jaime Schwender was the book's project editor. Her "five-star" editorial skills in concert with her good humor, gracious comments, and masterful scheduling are beyond compare. Her positive influence and professional attention clearly put her in a class of her own. Many thanks, too, to editor Julie Huggins for all her work and effort on my behalf. Matt Litts and Sarah Fannon are experts in publicity and have ensured an expansive and appreciative audience for this book. Cheers to them both. And editor Gregory McNamee's insightful direction brought coherence and vigor to every section of the manuscript. His scientific critiques, literary advice, and practical assistance ensured a sharp focus and clear purpose. Not only did his counsel increase the overall quality of this project, but he was also instrumental in helping promote a deep appreciation for these ancient wonders.

To you, dear reader, I offer my ultimate appreciation and acknowledgment. That you have sought information and insight into the lives of old trees is to be lauded. That you might use that knowledge to ensure the survival and preservation of these botanical wonders is, I hope, the ultimate message of these chapters. Trees have been our environmental partners long before our ancestors journeyed out of the Rift Valley to eventually populate every segment of the globe. As such, trees have been a commanding part of our lives, and we theirs. Knowledge of their ancestry, I believe, can help us ensure their appeal, and their extended presence, for future generations.

Thank you for your company.

References and Readings

The works listed here are those referred to in a designated chapter; that is, in the chapter where they are first quoted or to which they are most relevant. A work subsequently cited or quoted in an additional chapter is not listed again. For ease of reference, the sources are listed alphabetically rather than by their order within a chapter.

Preface

Berry, Christopher. "Paleobotany: The Rise of Earth's Early Forests." *Current Biology* (August 2019). https://www.sciencedirect.com/science/article/pii/S0960982219308619.

Boyer, Jamie. "Great Moments in Plant Evolution, Part 2: The Origin of Trees and Forests." Brooklyn Botanic Garden. https://www.bbg.org/news/great_moments_in_plant_evolution_part_2_the_origin_of_trees_and_forests.

Cassella, Carly. "This Ancient Tree Species is Virtually Immortal, and We Finally Understand How." *ScienceAlert* (January 14, 2020).

Greshko, Michael. "Huge Fossil Is Oldest Giant Flowering Tree in North America." National Geographic.com, September 26, 2018. https://www.nationalgeographic.com/science/article/news-petrified-log-utah-angiosperms-flowers-trees.

Kentucky Geological Survey. "Types of Trees Preserved as Fossil Tree Stumps." University of Kentucky. www.uky.edu/KGS/fossils/fossil-tree-stumps-types.

Martin, Anna. "Lifespan of Evergreen Trees—All Year Surprising Growth!" Embrace Gardening. www.embracegardening.com.

Meyer-Berthaud, Brigitte, Stephen Scheckler, and Jobst Wendt. "*Archaeopteris* Is the Earliest Known Modern Tree." *Nature* 398 (April 1999): 700–701.

Nash, Kira. "How Long Do Fruit Trees Live?" Tree Vitalize. https://treevitalize.com/how-long-do-fruit-trees-live/.

National Trust. "Ancient and Notable Trees." www.nationaltrust.org.uk/discover/nature/trees-plants/ancient-and-notable-trees.

O'Donoghue, James. "Primeval Forest: The Evolution of Trees." *New Scientist* 196, no. 2631 (November 24, 2007): 38–41.

Sussman, Rachel. *The Oldest Living Things in the World.* Chicago: University of Chicago Press, 2014.

Wang, Li, Jiawen Cui, Jinxing Lin, et al. "Multifeature Analysis of Vascular Cambial Cells Reveal Longevity Mechanisms in Old *Ginkgo biloba* Trees." *Biological Sciences* 117, no. 4 (January 13, 2020): 2201–10.

Woodland Trust. "Ancient Trees." www.woodlandtrust.org.uk/trees-woods-and -wildlife/british-trees/ancient-trees.

Introduction

Buettner, Dan. *The Blue Zones: 9 Lessons for Living Longer.* Washington, DC: National Geographic Society, 2008.

Bush, Evan. "Firmageddon: Researchers Find 1.1 Million Acres of Dead Trees in Oregon." NBC News.com, December 11, 2022.

Davis, Jack. *Gulf: The Making of an American Sea.* New York: Liveright, 2017.

Kolbert, Elizabeth. *The Sixth Extinction: An Unnatural History.* New York: Henry Holt, 2014.

Muir, John. *Steep Trails.* New York: Houghton Mifflin Company, 1918. www .gutenberg.org/ebooks/326.

Lopez, Barry. "The Passing Wisdom of Birds." In *Crossing Open Ground*, 193–208. New York: Vintage, 1988.

Raines, Ben. "Alabama's 60,000-Year-Old Underwater Forest Spills Its Secrets in New Documentary." www.al.com/news, June 25, 2017.

Satake, Alison. "Underwater Ancient Cypress Forest Offers Clues to the Past." Louisiana State University Media Center, June 3, 2021.

Stafford, Fiona. *The Long, Long Life of Trees.* New Haven, CT: Yale University Press, 2017.

St. George, Zach. *The Journeys of Trees: A Story about Forests, People, and the Future.* New York: Norton, 2020.

Stancil, Kenny. "'Wake-Up Call': NOAA Predicts One-Foot Sea-Level Rise by 2050." *Common Dreams*, February 15, 2022.

1. Old Warriors

Fredericks, Anthony D. *The Secret Life of Clams: The Mysteries and Magic of Our Favorite Shellfish.* New York: Skyhorse, 2014.

Lanner, Ronald M. *The Bristlecone Book: A Natural History of the World's Oldest Trees.* Missoula, MT: Mountain Press, 2007.

Lanner, Ronald M., and Kristina F. Conner. "Does Bristlecone Pine Senesce?" *Experimental Gerontology* 36 (2001): 675–85.

Lopez, Barry. *About This Life: Journeys on the Threshold of Memory.* New York: Random House, 2011.

Louth, John, and Kevin White. *Living History: The Ancient Bristlecone Pines.* DVD. USDA Forest Service/Eastern Sierra Interpretive Association, 2003.

Schlenz, Mark A. *A Day in the Ancient Bristlecone Pine Forest.* Bishop, CA: Companion Press, 2008.

Schulman, Edmund. "Bristlecone Pine, Oldest Known Living Thing." *National Geographic*, March 1958, 355–72.

Trouet, Valerie. *Tree Story: The History of the World Written in Rings.* Baltimore, MD: Johns Hopkins University Press, 2020.

2. Realm of the Old Man

Zhang, Quanchao, Xiaogang Hou, Shiyu Yang, Sunzifeng Ruan, Anqi Wang, Pengzhen Li, et al. "Eternal Love Locked in an Embrace and Sealed with a Ring: A Xianbei Couple's Joint Burial in North Wei Era, China (386–534 CE)." *International Journal of Osteoarchaeology* 31, no. 5 (June 4, 2021): 966–74. https://doi.org/10.1002/oa.3009.

3. Against a Crooked Sky

Budanovic, Nikola. "How a Geography Student Caused the Demise of a 4,900-Year-Old Tree." *The Vintage News*, July 4, 2018.

Iriarte, José, Irene Holst, Oscar Marozzi, Claudia Listopad, Eduardo Alonso, Andrés Rinderknecht, and Juan Montaña. "Evidence for Cultivar Adoption and Emerging Complexity during the mid-Holocene in the La Plata Basin." *Nature* 432 (December 2, 2004): 614–17.

Rutkow, Eric. *American Canopy: Trees, Forests, and the Making of a Nation.* New York: Scribners, 2012.

Tudge, Colin. *The Tree: A Natural History of What Trees Are, How They Live, and Why They Matter.* New York: Three Rivers Press, 2005.

4. Touching Clouds

Earle, Christopher J., ed. "*Sequoia sempervirens.*" The Gymnosperm Database. www.conifers.org.

Fredericks, Anthony D. *Tall Tall Tree*. Naperville, IL: Sourcebooks/Dawn Publications, 2017.

Hodder, Sam, et al. *The Once and Future Forest: California's Iconic Redwoods*. Berkeley, CA: Heyday Books, 2018.

Preston, Richard. *The Wild Trees: A Story of Passion and Daring*. New York: Random House, 2007.

Rohde, Jerry, and Gisela Rohde. *Best Short Hikes in Redwood National and State Parks*. Seattle, WA: Mountaineers Books, 2004.

"The Tallest Tree in the World/Hyperion, the World's Tallest Living Tree." *Monumental Trees*. www.monumentaltrees.com/en/trees/coastredwood/tallest_tree_in_the_world.

Wei-Haas, Maya. "Mummy Yields Earliest Known Egyptian Embalming Recipe." National Geographic.com, August 15, 2018. https://www.nationalgeographic.com/science/article/news-egyptian-prehistoric-mummy-embalming-recipe.

Wohlleben, Peter. *The Hidden Life of Trees: What They Feel, How They Communicate—Discoveries from a Secret World*. Vancouver, BC: Greystone Books, 2016.

5. Kayaking through Time

Georgiou, Aristos. "2,624-Year-Old Tree Discovered in North Carolina Swamp Is One of the Oldest on Earth." *Newsweek*, May 10, 2019.

Hempton, Gordon. *One Square Inch of Silence: One Man's Search for Natural Silence in a Noisy World*. New York: Free Press, 2009.

Horan, Jack. "River of Time: The Stunning Old-Growth Forest in the Three Sisters Swamp." *Coastwatch*, Autumn 2019. https://ncseagrant.ncsu.edu/coastwatch/current-issue/autumn-2019/river-of-time/.

Li, Qing. *Forest Bathing: How Trees Can Help You Find Health and Happiness*. New York: Viking, 2018.

Münzel, Thomas, Mette Sørensen, Frank Schmidt, Erwin Schmidt, Sebastian Steven, Swenja Kröller-Schön, and Andreas Daiber. "The Adverse Effects of Environmental Noise Exposure on Oxidative Stress and Cardiovascular Risk." *Antioxidants & Redox Signaling* 28, no. 9 (2018): 873–908. doi:10.1089/ars.2017.7118.

Smith, Laurence C. *Rivers of Power: How a Natural Force Raised Kingdoms, Destroyed Civilizations, and Shapes Our World*. New York: Little, Brown, 2020.

Stahle, D. W., J. R. Edmondson, I. M. Howard, C. R. Robbins, R. D. Griffin, A. Carl, C. B. Hall, and M. C. A. Torbenson. "Longevity, Climate Sensitivity, and Conservation Status of Wetland Trees at Black River, North Carolina." *Environmental Research Communications* 1, no. 4 (May 9, 2019). https://doi.org/10.1088/2515-7620/ab0c4a.

6. Beyond Memory

"Aspen Ecology." US Forest Service. www.fs.fed.us/wildflowers/beauty/aspen
/ecology.shtml.

Bauman, Joe. "Ice Age in Utah." *Deseret News*, December 3, 1997.

Friends of Pando. www.friendsofpando.org.

Nace, Trevor. "The World's Largest Organism, Pando, Is Dying." Forbes.com,
October 18, 2018. https://www.forbes.com/sites/trevornace/2018/10/18/the
-worlds-largest-organism-pando-is-dying/?sh=7e1b47de5554.

Wang, Yuchang, Mikkel Winther Pedersen, Inger Greve Alsos, Bianca De Sanctis,
Fernando Racimo, Ana Prohaska, et al. "Late Quaternary Dynamics of Arctic
Biota from Ancient Environmental Genomics." *Nature* 600 (2021): 86–92.

7. Giants of the Sierras

Cartwright, Mark. "Olmec Colossal Stone Heads." World History Encyclopedia.
https://www.worldhistory.org/article/672/olmec-colossal-stone-heads/.

Louv, Richard. *Last Child in the Woods: Saving Our Children From Nature-Deficit
Disorder.* Chapel Hill, NC: Algonquin Books, 2005.

National Park Service. "Giant Sequoias and Fire." Sequoia and Kings Canyon
National Parks. www.nps.gov/seki/learn/nature/giant-sequoias-and-fire.htm.

"Oldest Redwood Trees in United States." Oldest.org. www.oldest.org/nature
/redwood-trees-us.

Quammen, David. "Forest Giant." NationalGeographic.com, December 2012.
https://www.nationalgeographic.com/magazine/article/giant-sequoias.

Turner, Scott. *Hike the Parks: Sequoia & Kings Canyon National Parks.* Seattle,
WA: Mountaineers Books, 2020.

Tweed, William C. *King Sequoia: The Tree That Inspired a Nation, Created Our
National Park System, and Changed the Way We Think about Nature.* Berkeley,
CA: Heyday Books, 2016.

8. Prehistoric Roots

"The Jurupa Oak—Third Oldest Living Thing on Earth." *Los Angeles Almanac*,
May 25, 2019.

May, Michael, Mitchell Provance, Andrew Sanders, Norman Ellstrand, and Jeffrey
Ross-Ibarra. "A Pleistocene Clone of Palmer's Oak Persisting in Southern
California." *PLOS One*, December 23, 2009. https://doi.org/10.1371/journal.pone
.0008346.

Nicholson, Uisdean, Veronica Bray, Sean Gulick, and Benedict Aduomahor. "The Nadir Crater Offshore West Africa: A Candidate Cretaceous-Paleogene Impact Structure." *Science Advances* 8, no. 33 (August 17, 2022). https://doi.org/10.1126/sciadv.abn3096.

Stickel, E. Gary. *Why the Original Indian Tribe of the Greater Los Angeles Area Is Called Kizh Not Tongva.* San Gabriel, CA: Kizh Tribal Press, 2016.

Torchinsky, Rina. "Cristina Calderón, Chile's Last Known Yaghan Speaker, Dies at 93." NPR.org, February 18, 2022. https://www.npr.org/2022/02/18/1081584395/cristina-calderon-chiles-last-known-yaghan-speaker-dies-at-93.

Yong, Ed. "The 13,000-Year Old Tree That Survives by Cloning Itself." *National Geographic*, December 2009.

9. Sequestered Icon

Lopez, Barry. "Yukon-Charley: The Shape of Wilderness." In *Crossing Open Ground*, 73–92. New York: Random House, 1989.

Mother Lode Land Trust. "Bennett Juniper." November 30, 2022. https://motherlodelandtrust.org/mllt-blog.

Romey, Kristin. "3,600-Year-Old Tsunami 'Time Capsule' Sheds Light on One of Humanity's Greatest Disasters." NationalGeographic.com, December 27, 2021. https://www.nationalgeographic.com/history/article/3600-year-old-tsunami-time-capsule-sheds-light-on-one-of-humanitys-greatest-disasters.

Save the Redwoods League. "Bennett Juniper Stewardship Project." www.savetheredwoods.org/project/bennett-juniper-stewardship-project.

Smith, Kiona. "First Victim of the Tsunami That Trashed the Eastern Mediterranean Found." Ars Technica, January 5, 2022. https://arstechnica.com/science/2022/01/archaeologists-find-victim-of-ancient-tsunami-caused-by-thera-eruption/.

Treeographer. "The Bennett Juniper—America's Oldest Juniper Tree." November 8, 2017. https://thetreeographer.com/2017/11/08/the-bennett-juniper-americas-oldest-juniper-tree.

10. Sight to See

Guion, William. "Most Magnificent Louisiana Live Oak: Seven Sisters Oak." *Country Roads Magazine*, July 2, 2013.

Louisiana Garden Club Federation. "Live Oak Society." www.lgcfinc.org/live-oak-society.html.

National Wildlife Federation. "Southern Live Oak." www.nwf.org/Educational
-Resources/Wildlife-Guide/Plants-and-Fungi/Southern-Live-Oak.

Conclusion

Alanna, Eloise. "The Ancient Trees at the Heart of a Case Against the Crown." BBC
News, January 25, 2023.

American Forests. www.americanforests.org.

Archangel Ancient Tree Archive. www.ancienttreearchive.org.

Cannon, Charles H., Gianluca Piovesan, and Sergi Munné-Bosch. "Old and
Ancient Trees Are Life History Lottery Winners and Vital Evolutionary
Resources for Long-Term Adaptive Capacity." *Nature Plants* 8 (January 31,
2022): 136–45.

Crable, Ad. "Quest Under Way to Find, Protect Old-Growth Forests." *Bay Journal*,
December 17, 2021.

Diamond, Jonny. "The Old Man and the Tree." *Smithsonian Magazine*, January/
February 2022.

Loader, Neil J., Danny McCarroll, Daniel Miles, Giles H. F. Young, Darren Davies,
and Christopher Bronk Ramsey. "Tree Ring Dating Using Oxygen Isotopes:
A Master Chronology for Central England." *Journal of Quaternary Science* 34,
no. 6 (2019): 475–90. https://doi.org/10.1002/jqs.3115.

Old Growth Forest Network. www.oldgrowthforest.net.

Pitts, Jonathan M. "Steady Growth: Maryland Woman Spearheads Fight to Preserve
America's Old-Growth Forests." *Baltimore Sun*, March 13, 2022.

Index